TALES FROM A T-BALL OUTFIELD

Kim & Jason

4

TALES FROM A T-BALL OUTFIELD: KIM & JASON ANNUAL #4

ISBN-10: 0-9715253-4-X
ISBN-13: 978-0-9715253-4-4

Follow the adventures of Kim & Jason online at
http://www.KimandJason.com
Sign up to get Kim & Jason in your inbox!

Send Jason Kotecki e-mail at: jbird@jbirdink.com.

This book is dedicated to Joel Dawson, who always believed in me and coached the game in which I got my first win as a pitcher.

Kim and Jason are two characters from the mind of artist Jason Kotecki. They inhabit the comic strip by the same name and navigate a sea of adventures as they try to make straight the crooked world of grown-ups. By combining the gifts of art and humor, the strip and its lively characters evoke smiles on the faces of readers and stir the childlike spirit within. It all began when the real-life Jason met the real-life Kim way back in 1995. It wasn't long before the two realized they shared a kindred childlike spirit. One day, Jason sketched himself and his girlfriend as young cartoon characters, and they began appearing on all kinds of homemade cards and gifts designed to win her heart. Jason's efforts were not in vain, as the couple was married in May 2000. Since then, the characters have taken on lives of their own and the "real" Kim and Jason have built a company (JBiRD iNK) to promote and distribute the comic strip and its inspiring message.

So return to a time when agendas were made up as you went along, meetings were held in your living room under a tent made of couch cushions and blankets, and candy was more valuable than any mutual fund. Take a moment to slip back into a world where truth, hope, and imagination are always alive.

WHAT PAPER ARE YOU IN? That's the question I'm inevitably asked each time I tell someone that I do a comic strip. (Other than, "How do you come up with your ideas?") I can't blame people for asking because that's where comic strips belong, right? As of this writing, I can confidently say that we're in about twenty papers – and about 100 smaller newsletters – as if that somehow justifies me as legitimate. Does a comic strip need to be in a newspaper to be legitimate – or profitable?

I also get asked how the "Syndicate Game" works. How, exactly, do you get IN papers? Since most editors prefer to work through a syndicate, here are the basics in a nutshell:

1) Cartoonist creates a comic strip.
2) Cartoonist sends six weeks worth of strips to one of the dwindling number of major syndicates left.
3) Cartoonist waits four months to hear something back. In the meantime, the syndicate sifts through thousands of mostly amateurish submissions. Of the other hundred remaining, the syndicate eliminates the ones that are too controversial, too plain, too much like a strip they already have, not enough like a strip they already have, and the ones they don't figure will make a million dollars in five years.
4a) Cartoonist finally receives a form letter politely thanking said cartoonist for his submission, but regrettably, blah, blah, blah... (OR)...
4b) Cartoonist receives a letter or call of praise saying the syndicate LOVES the strip, but wants the cartoonist to change this, that, and oh, by the way, the title.

A few years ago, I submitted *Kim & Jason* to the syndicates, and got the standard rejection letter. In retrospect, they made the right call. There were a lot of things to iron out, and the art was very inconsistent. Last year, I actually spoke with a syndicate big wig, who gave me an honest critique. She really liked the art, but encouraged me to work on the writing, which she felt could be funnier. However, she also admitted that the strip might be too "sweet" for generally cynical newspaper editors. Since then, I've committed myself to beefing up the writing, and am sometimes pleased with the results. And every six months or so, I find myself asking the question: Are the syndicates for me?

It started years ago with the first submissions. The rejection letters forced me to make a decision: Would I give up, or try and make it without them? Obviously, I chose the latter, figuring that if I could build a big enough audience, the syndicates would take notice and ultimately, sign me to a contract. The audience has grown ever since and the comic strip, I believe, has gotten increasingly better. It has taken lots and lots of WORK...not to mention a little blood (X-acto knives are sharp), sweat, and tears.

As the strip improves, readership grows, and more retail stores carry our products, I can't help but wonder: Do we NEED the syndicates? Common knowledge says yes, but the rebellious, visionary, entrepreneur in me says, "Heck no!"

The rebellious side of me (which is also quite stubborn) says, "You've had your chance - and you passed on the opportunity of a lifetime! I'll show you!" (A bit presumptuous and conceited, I'll admit, but I like to think the great ones often displayed this attitude.)

The visionary side of me sees a declining status quo. Fifteen, or even ten years ago, it would have been impossible for me to be doing what I'm able to do now. *Kim & Jason* is available to a worldwide audience. Technology has wrought many changes and people's habits are changing with it. The power the syndicates once wielded is declining. Newspapers are dying, as more and more people get their news from cable TV and the Web.

The entrepreneur in me sees a boatload of opportunities available to someone with a little creativity and a willingness to work hard. The syndicates are a big business, and big businesses habitually make "safe" decisions, and often miss great opportunities. They have their connections and all, but I have a hard time stomaching the idea of them getting half of everything after all the hard work we've put in marketing this thing.

So the inner debate continues. Right now, my company JBiRD iNK syndicates *Kim & Jason*. We have a nice, easy system set up for newspaper editors who would like to add K&J to their comic sections. While I'd certainly love the connections and scope the syndicates could offer (if they even would want *Kim & Jason* at all), I believe in my heart that as time moves forward and our audience grows, those same syndicates will have less and less to offer us. We'll see. For now, I'll keep telling folks what papers we're in to ease their minds that *Kim & Jason* is a real comic strip, while quietly working at making the syndicates irrelevant.

In the meantime, *Kim & Jason* rolls on. This book in your hands marks four years and counting... thanks for reading!

Jason

THE CAST

"I'M DEFINITELY GONNA BECOME A PILOT BEFORE I BECOME PRESIDENT."

KIM is a spunky little girl who is a bundle of innocence, unabashed confidence, and hopeless naiveté. She has the ability to pare down complex issues into tidy and logical, albeit misguided explanations. Her carefree attitude guides her through life and her stubbornness sometimes gets the better of her. Her most prized possession is a stuffed skunk named Stinky, a gift from Boompa.

"I WISH THEY'D TEAR DOWN THE MALL AND PUT UP A JUNGLE."

JASON is a little boy with hair that's as wild as his imagination. Kim's best friend is smart, shy and anxious, and usually enveloped in a world of dreams and fantasy. He can often be seen saving the world from evil as Super J, a fearless, 3D goggled superhero with supreme confidence. His hero is the fictional swashbuckling space smuggler from Star Warriors fame, Ace Laser.

"PUKE BAGS, HAVE WE NO PUKE BAGS?"

STINKY is Kim's favorite stuffed animal, who just happens to be a skunk. Although inanimate and unable to communicate audibly, Stinky has a remarkably distinguished taste and outlook on life. A connoisseur of the English language, gourmet food, and the finer things in life, he has an opinion on pretty much everything. Despite his mature perspective, nothing clouds his loyalty to Kim. Stinky reeks of Old Spice, which was applied by Kim in an attempt to get him to smell more skunk-like.

"I'M ON THE PHONE!!!"

KATIE is Kim's seventh grade older sister. To Kim and Jason, she is evil incarnate, the quintessential older sibling who knows everything and tells all. Usually annoyed by her younger sister, Katie is wrapped up in her world – a world of boys, school, and volleyball. For some reason, she seems to thrive on making life miserable for Kim and her friend, never hesitating to take the passive-aggressive cheap shot or manipulating them to do her will. There are moments of civility between the sisters, albeit short-lived.

"BA GAA BOO BA."

DOUGIE is Jason's younger brother. He mumbles garbled sentences and is often an annoyance to Kim and particularly Jason, although they occasionally like to amuse themselves with him. Dougie likes to eat stuff, preferably things made of plastic and owned by Jason.

"PEOPLE WITH CLEAN ROOMS HAVE HIGHER CHANCES OF EATING ICE CREAM."

BOOMPA is a wise and witty senior who provides answers to some of life's most challenging questions. A retired carpenter with a heart of gold, Kim's grandfather is always giving the kids gifts and explaining how things work. He is old enough to know the wisdom that children possess, and always takes time to honor their questions, stories, and ramblings. Despite a lifetime of experiences, Boompa has not yet outgrown his childhood.

THE EPISODES

THE PIGGY BANK

I really enjoy exploring the inner workings of a child's mind, especially how they view the things that grown-ups take for granted. I've noticed that if you make a habit of looking at things from a child's viewpoint, it doesn't take long to start seeing how absurd the "grown-up world" really is. This episode also reminds me of how much I miss the days when a handful of quarters, nickels, and dimes felt like the booty from an abandoned pirate ship.

Whatcha doin?
Counting my money. You can help.
www.KimandJason.com © 2003 by Jason W. Kotecki
Only if I get ten percent.
No way.
KOTECKI
Okay, I guess I'll do it pro bono.
Fine, as long as you do it for free.

Where'd you get all this money?
Birthdays, allowance, the usual.
How come you haven't spent it?
I haven't decided how.
Plus, I can't drive and I don't have a credit card.
KOTECKI
www.KimandJason.com © 2003 by Jason W. Kotecki
Whoever said "money is power" was a grown-up.

WOAH! Where did you get all these dimes?
Oh, I ripped off Katie...
www.KimandJason.com © 2003 by Jason W. Kotecki
She gave me TWO dimes for every quarter I gave her!
What a sucker!
I felt bad at first, but I figured it makes up for all the times she tricked me.
KOTECKI

So, don't you have any money at home?
A little, but I usually blow it right away.
I live allowance to allowance.
It's tough to get ahead.
Especially when they keep raising the price of Jawbreakers.
www.KimandJason.com © 2003 by Jason W. Kotecki
kotecki

WOW! Seven dollars and thirty six cents!
Do you think it's enough for a pony?
I don't know... I can't imagine them for less than ten bucks.
Really?
Unless the pony has a high plastic content and hails from Taiwan.
www.KimandJason.com © 2003 by Jason W. Kotecki
kotecki

Childhood Is... Piggy Banks.

Do grown-ups have piggy banks?
Yeah, but theirs are bigger.
And people work inside.
BANK
kotecki

> "I live allowance to allowance."

IN GOD WE TRUST
LIBERTY
2003
I wonder why nickels are bigger than dimes, but dimes are worth more?
I'm pretty sure the guy on the nickel had a bigger head than the guy on the dime.
www.KimandJason.com © 2003 by Jason W. Kotecki
Well how come pennies are brown, but all the other coins are silver?
Brown was Abeham Lincoln's favorite color.
And pennies would have been a lot bigger, but they prob'ly made him take off his big hat when they took his picture.
Good thing they did that...
Otherwise, pennies wouldn't fit into vending machines.
Or penny loafers!
kotecki

THE PILOT

The real-life Kim's real-life father has always been quite fond of airplanes. Air shows have been a big part of Kim's family for as long as she can remember. Probably due to this influence, when she was younger, Kim dreamed of becoming a pilot. I finally got a chance to really explore this side of Kim's character with this episode. Stinky became the first victim – I mean passenger – to fly on *Kim Air*.

Let's go, Stinky!
Finally, a reprieve from this tortured middle-class existence.
www.KimandJason.com © 2003 by Jason W. Kotecki
We're going to fly the friendly skies!
I hear New Zealand is beautiful this time of year.
Oh...
I have a sneaky suspicion that this flight doesn't serve mixed drinks.
No more room for you, Mr. Parachute!
kotecki

Stinky Speaks

Don't you hate it when you board a flight and you immediately realize you should have updated your will and life insurance policy?

I've never really flown before.
No! I refuse to believe it!
www.KimandJason.com © 2003 by Jason W. Kotecki
Unless you count that one time at Pizza Pete's...
But that was just a ride you put tokens in...
But of course, that's just pretend! This is...
And it didn't have as much horsepower as THIS baby!
...something else.
kotecki

Stinky Speaks

This oughta be good. I try to encourage. I'm nothing if not an advocate for encouragement, but I wonder how long this will last.

Trading Spaces is almost on and Vern's one of the designers.

Ready for take-off, co-pilot Stinky?
Can I use my cell phone yet?
kotecki
What the...?
www.KimandJason.com © 2003 by Jason W. Kotecki
Pretty nice view, huh?
Puke bags! Have we no puke bags?

Stinky Speaks

Oh yeah, this goes down as one of the worst things I've ever experienced. Not quite as bad as the time I sampled the zesty metallic aftertaste of a chrome bumper when hurtling down a hill on that ill-fated luge run.

But then again, this little trip isn't over yet, and I still can't find a usable vomit receptacle.

Okay, co-pilot Stinky, we're gonna do some tricks!
This isn't it?
www.KimandJason.com © 2003 by Jason W. Kotecki
Uh-oh.
kotecki
Je serai bientôt une crêpe de skunk.
{Translation: I shall soon be a skunk pancake.}

Stinky Speaks

Oui je parle français. Avez-vous un parachute?

[Translation: Yes I speak French. Do you have a parachute?]

kotecki
VROOOM
www.KimandJason.com © 2003 by Jason W. Kotecki
Stinky, I'm sorry you fell out of my plane!
God? Is that you?
I thought you were wearing the seatbelt.
My... heaven never looked this dirty on TV...

Stinky Speaks

Où sont les anges? Où sont les portes nacrées? Où Est Michael Landon?

[Translation: Where are the angels? Where are the pearly gates? Where's Michael Landon?]

“Puke bags! Have we no puke bags?”

Childhood Is... An Open Mind.
It's a super-fast fighter plane!
It's a secret space portal to Mars!
I see a cardboard box that once housed a now little-used kitchen appliance...But I'm a purist.
kotecki www.KimandJason.com © 2003 by Jason W. Kotecki

kotecki
www.KimandJason.com © 2003 by Jason W. Kotecki
Hey, where's the mail?
Sorry, it was out of my way.

Do you want to go for a ride in my plane?
Ride at your own risk.
Okay!
You're taking your life into your own hands!
Stinky was my first passenger.
kotecki
www.KimandJason.com © 2003 by Jason W. Kotecki
Victim is more like it!
You'll prob'ly need a helmet.

Stinky Speaks

A helmet? A helmet!? If that's all you need, you better pick one out that looks good at a funeral, because you'll be wearing it in your casket. The only reason I'm still here is because skunks have 19 lives.

Here's my plane!
COOL!
A two-seater, huh?
Yep, pretty much.
www.KimandJason.com © 2003 by Jason W. Kotecki
You'll have to stay here this time, Stinky.
What, and miss out on all the bodily harm?
kotecki

Stinky Speaks

When I woke up this morning I had a strong suspicion that this would be my lucky day. No, I'm not the newest 20 million dollar lottery winner, but at least I know I won't be spending the next three months of my life in a hospital bed watching *Diff'rent Strokes* re-runs sipping my salad through a straw.

Seatbelts?
Check.
kotecki
Headgear?
Check.
RUMBLE
RUMBLE
Imagination?
Check.
www.KimandJason.com © 2003 by Jason W. Kotecki
Hey – I forgot my passport!

Wow! This plane rules!
Not a bad view, huh?
I'll say...
www.KimandJason.com © 2003 by Jason W. Kotecki
I can't believe how little every-thing looks!
Yeah, but it's weird that we can't see any of those words they show on the map.
Kotecki

This is the life!
Soaring above the clouds, away from all the stress of life.
Leaving behind all the monotonous daily hassles and pressures.
www.KimandJason.com © 2003 by Jason W. Kotecki
Not that I have any of those.
Kotecki

Can't you pass this jerk? He's not even going the speed limit!
I don't know where these people learn to fly...
Kotecki
www.KimandJason.com © 2003 by Jason W. Kotecki

Childhood Is... Lofty Ambitions.

Next stop–
New Jersey!
Kotecki www.KimandJason.com
© 2003 by Jason W. Kotecki

So, does this plane do tricks?
www.KimandJason.com © 2003 by Jason W. Kotecki
Barrel roll.
Oh man, I just put ON these underpants!
kotecki

WOOSH
kotecki
How'd you learn to fly this fast?
It runs in the family.
I didn't know your Dad flew planes...
He doesn't, but you should see him drive when he's in a hurry!
www.KimandJason.com © 2003 by Jason W. Kotecki

kotecki
GREAT! I got cloud up my nose!
www.KimandJason.com © 2003 by Jason W. Kotecki

The world looks so neat up here!
kotecki
I guess that's why people want to go to heaven...
www.KimandJason.com © 2003 by Jason W. Kotecki
It's got the best view.
I hear the food's good, too.

kotecki
Uh oh.
PUT PUT PITTER SPUT
www.KimandJason.com © 2003 by Jason W. Kotecki
This is what I get for flying coach.

"Oh man, I just put ON these underpants!"

Childhood Is... A Fresh Perspective.

If they built planes out of cheese, no one would get hurt if they crash!
kotecki
www.KimandJason.com © 2003 by Jason W. Kotecki

Hmmm. Now there's something you don't see every day...
kotecki
www.KimandJason.com © 2003 by Jason W. Kotecki

kotecki
Oh man, what happened?
I think we ran out of gas.
I can't believe we're not dead!
Thank good-ness.
www.KimandJason.com © 2003 by Jason W. Kotecki
I'm expecting Heaven to have a bunch of singing people and **A LOT** more chocolate!

Your plane looks totalled.
It doesn't look good.
kotecki
The important thing is that we're safe and we find our way home.
www.KimandJason.com © 2003 by Jason W. Kotecki
But not too fast. It's my night to set the table.

Our plane has crashed and we have no idea where we are – what's the plan?
Relax – don't panic, I saw this on TV once...
kotecki
www.KimandJason.com © 2003 by Jason W. Kotecki
Well, what should we do?
QUICK! Grab some duct tape and mozzarella cheese!

I wonder what strange place we landed in.
www.KimandJason.com © 2003 by Jason W. Kotecki
Maybe we're on Mars.
REALLY? I think I have a map for that!
Nope. This is Minnesota.
kotecki

By holding these sticks together, we can pick up radio signals. Maybe they'll lead us home!
www.KimandJason.com © 2003 by Jason W. Kotecki
Hear that? Let's move closer to the source...
JASON! SUPPER'S READY! GET YOUR BUTT IN HERE!
Hey – we're home! It worked!
Loud and clear.
kotecki

Childhood Is... Onion Precautions.

Dougie, promise me that if this has onions in it and I die, you'll report Mom to the authorities.
Gaa!
www.KimandJason.com © 2003 by Jason W. Kotecki
kotecki

I learned all the important things in life from my Dad.
How to dress appropriately.
How to fix things.
scritch
How to ask for directions.
How to cook.
kotecki
www.KimandJason.com © 2003 by Jason W. Kotecki
Happy 50th, Dad!

THE SLEEPOVER

The treehouse that Boompa built several episodes ago comes back into play in this one. Thanks to mean ol' Katie, Jason's anxiousness comes into play as well. I was quite the scaredy cat when I was a kid, which obviously translates well into the "character" of Jason. Of course I am no longer afraid of ghosts now that I'm grown. Well, except for the kind that eat your kidneys.

This treehouse **RULES!**
kotecki
www.KimandJason.com © 2003 by Jason W. Kotecki
This is exactly how I want my house to be when I grow up!
It might be nice if it had one of those hi-def plasma TVs.
Of course. I just figured that went without saying!

You know what would be cool?
www.KimandJason.com © 2003 by Jason W. Kotecki
If we had a giant water slide that led to a big pool of wet spaghetti?
kotecki
No...
I was thinking we could sleep here overnight.
Oh.
So no spaghetti?

Boompa, can we sleep in the tree-house tonight?
kotecki
www.KimandJason.com © 2003 by Jason W. Kotecki
I don't see why not, but I'll have to ask your parents.
Just a tip: before you ask them, make sure they're in a good mood.
And your chores are done!

Well kids, your parents said it was okay...
You can stay overnight in the treehouse.
YIPPEE!
YES
I hope my Mom's OK. It's my first night away from home.
Judging by the number of backflips she did, I think she'll be fine.
My Mom can do backflips?
kotecki
www.KimandJason.com © 2003 by Jason W. Kotecki

Don't you have a sleeping bag?
Good idea. I can get this down the hall, but there's no way this baby's going in the treehouse.
kotecki
www.KimandJason.com © 2003 by Jason W. Kotecki

This place could use some improvements!
Yeah, I was thinking about a moat.
Do they sell alligators at Home Depot?
kotecki
www.KimandJason.com © 2003 by Jason W. Kotecki

"Do they sell alligators at Home Depot?"

Childhood Is...
Secret Hideouts.
This is an ingenious design!
I know - kids can get in, but grown-ups can't!
www.KimandJason.com © 2003 by Jason W. Kotecki
kotecki

Do we have everything we need to sleep in the treehouse?
Sleeping bags, pillows, Easy Bake Oven...
Easy Bake Oven?
Well, my Mom already said no to the TV, I doubt we'll score the grill!
www.KimandJason.com © 2003 by Jason W. Kotecki
kotecki

TOP 5 LIST OF THINGS REQUESTED (AND DENIED) FOR THE TREEHOUSE OVERNIGHT ADVENTURE...

1. The hi-def big screen TV.
2. Kim's Dad's La-Z-Boy recliner.
3. Kim's Mom's La-Z-Boy recliner.
4. Boompa's pool table.
5. A swimming pool filled with cooked spaghetti.

If we're sleeping overnight in the treehouse, we'll need a flashlight.
Katie has one.
Good–go ask her for it.
No... maybe you should.
But she's **YOUR** sister.
Trust me. Me and a ballerina from a broken music box both think **YOU** should ask her.
www.KimandJason.com © 2003 by Jason W. Kotecki
Kotecki

Um...Katie, can I borrow your flashlight?
Whatever, why?
Me and Kim are sleeping over in the tree-house!
And you think a flashlight will be enough to scare the ghosts?
Ghosts?
Here, at least take this tennis racket. Aim for the kneecaps.
www.KimandJason.com © 2003 by Jason W. Kotecki
Kotecki

KATIE'S DIARY

I really pulled one over on the twerps today. That Jason asked to borrow my flashlight because they're sleeping out in Boompa's treehouse or something. I got him all scared about ghosts and stuff.

He looked like he was gonna pee his pants. They're like, so gullible.

It's fun to mess with them, but I have more important things to worry about. Like who Chad has a crush on and who broke the ballerina off my music box..."

We have a problem.
Katie said there's ghosts in the treehouse.
She's prob'ly lying. I'm not going to think about it. I'm not even going to tell Kim.
THERE'S GHOSTS IN THE TREEHOUSE!
Kotecki
www.KimandJason.com © 2003 by Jason W. Kotecki

Katie said there are ghosts in the tree-house?
Yeah! And she gave me this tennis racket to whack 'em!
I don't know... Maybe we shouldn't sleep out there tonight...
Kotecki
Relax. We'll be fine. I'll bring Stinky for protection.
That doesn't make me feel any better.
Oh, and I LIKE sleeping on wooden planks and being an all-you-can-eat mosquito buffet.
www.KimandJason.com © 2003 by Jason W. Kotecki

I've been thinking about what I want to do with my life.
I've decided I'm going to be a Mom **AFTER** I'm done being a famous drummer.
And I'm definitely going to become a pilot **BEFORE** I become President.
That way I can fly to my inaugimation.
And if I promise to wipe out broccoli, who **WOULDN'T** vote for me?
I'd vote for you no matter what!
I'm just not sure if there's enough room on the White House roof for a biplane.
Kotecki
www.KimandJason.com © 2003 by Jason W. Kotecki

Childhood Is... Not Cynicism.

Well, that's true. Adults do have sole custody of that one. But all we need is a positive attitude. And less politicians.
www.KimandJason.com © 2003 by Jason W. Kotecki
Kotecki

This is it! Our first night in the treehouse!
Hilton, eat your heart out.
Let's get settled!
What? No mint on my plank?
www.KimandJason.com © 2003 by Jason W. Kotecki
Kotecki

Stinky Speaks

These accommodations are ridiculous. I wouldn't ask my worst enemy to stay in a dump like this. No electricity, no indoor plumbing, no chenille velvet comforters? How can I expect to survive in a place this desolate? Of course, to the kids, this place is a palace. But I've never seen a palace with such disregard for modern comfort and complimentary velour robes!

This place is nice–just like home.
What, are you still worried about ghosts?
Katie's a big fat liar. And we have Stinky, remember?
To be fair, I may be a judo juggernaut, but I've never jousted with the undead...
www.KimandJason.com © 2003 by Jason W. Kotecki
Kotecki

Stinky Speaks

It's true. I am nothing short of an expert in judo. I don't usually talk much about it, but I used to be able to take down an offensive lineman without so much as breaking a sweat. It's been a few years, so I'm likely quite rusty, but I can still hold my own. If you're looking for someone to topple ghouls and such, I'd call Peter Venkman, as I wasn't awarded a proton pack with my black belt.

Hey kids - are you all settled in?
www.KimandJason.com © 2003 by Jason W. Kotecki
Jason thinks we'll see ghosts.
That's nonsense.
I know. I TOLD him Stinky would take 'em out.
I'm the Stinkinator.
kotecki

Stinky Speaks Yes, I'm the Stinkinator. I considered running for governor of California, but I don't have a German accent and I didn't appear in any 80's sitcoms with Mr. Drummond.

This popcorn is okay, but you know what would be GREAT?
If they'd cover it with chocolate or caramel or something.
They do. You can buy them at the store.
REALLY. Well why doesn't my Mom buy it?
WAIT. Can you buy mashed potatoes with marshmallows on them, too?
www.KimandJason.com © 2003 by Jason W. Kotecki
kotecki

Stinky Speaks And people give ME a hard time when I ask for ants on my pizza?

Do you know any scary stories?
Not really...my Dad doesn't read me those else I'll get nightmares.
www.KimandJason.com © 2003 by Jason W. Kotecki
Anyone heard the one about the guy who always wore striped ties with plaid shirts?
Frightening.
kotecki

Stinky Speaks Seriously, I've never seen anyone in my life more in need of a field trip to Nieman Marcus. And while I'm at it, when did old guys ever decide it would be a good idea to wear dress shoes and socks with their white shorts? It terrifies me just to think about it.

Childhood Is...
Camping Outside.
I wish we had a bonfire to roast these.
I wonder if your Boompa has matches.
Or a fire engine in his garage.
www.KimandJason.com © 2003 by Jason W. Kotecki
kotecki

Stinky Speaks

It's a shame we're without matches. Nothing embodies autumn quite like the burnt umbery bouquet of slightly roasted treehouse.

I like sleeping out in this treehouse.
It's what they call getting "back to basics".
I'd like to get back to my waterbed.
kotecki

Z
Z
Z
Kim, wake up! Did you hear that?
Whaa...?
www.KimandJason.com © 2003 by Jason W. Kotecki
I think I hear a ghost outside!
That's the wind.
No, it's whispers.
Unless it's selling beauty sleep in a bottle, tell it to keep it down.
kotecki

Not only is my side sore from sleeping on treated lumber, but now I can't even get a minute's worth of shut-eye thanks to these two kids jibber-jabbering about ethereal beings. My positive attitude reminds me that it could always be worse. At least I'm not surrounded by a gaggle of giggling twelve-year-old girls at a sleep over after the first full week of school. Yikes.

Stinky Speaks

Hear that? It's the ghost!
snap
It sounds like it's getting closer.
But don't worry, we've got Stinky!
Stinky, keep the ghosts away.
kotecki
www.KimandJason.com © 2003 by Jason W. Kotecki
Um... shoo?

Stinky Speaks

I must admit, spooking specters is not really my bag. But the kids don't seem to notice. Frankly, I often feel my ability to distinguish various vintages of Dom Perignon from the past thirty years also goes unnoticed.

I thought you said Stinky would protect us from ghosts!...
kotecki
...It's still out there!
Perhaps I'm too handsome to be a deterrant.
KNOCK
KNOCK
KNOCK
www.KimandJason.com © 2003 by Jason W. Kotecki
We're doomed! It'll eat our kidneys!
AHHH

Stinky Speaks

I knew it. My striking good looks serve as a disadvantage yet again. Who could possibly be frightened by a specimen this fine? Alas, I shall carry on, undeterred by this weighty cross that I bear...

This is it! You shine the light in the ghost's eyes and I'll drop popcorn on it!
RATTLE RATTLE
kotecki
HEY KIDS
www.KimandJason.com © 2003 by Jason W. Kotecki
BOOMPA!
Did you get the ghost? Did you see where it went?

Stinky Speaks

Hmpf. Turns out the "ghost" was really just Kim's grandfather...or was it? Are you kidding me? Of course it was. Or was it?... Sorry. Just trying to add a little drama here. As I see it, the biggest tragedy of all is that gourmet popcorn uneaten and ruined lying everywhere. Since when is popcorn a phantom repellent?

There aren't ANY ghosts, kids.
www.KimandJason.com © 2003 by Jason W. Kotecki
But we heard one walking around and whispering.
I think it was after our kidneys.
The only one out here is ME.
Well...can we sleep at your house...just in case?
I call the La-Z-Boy!
kotecki

Stinky Speaks

Finally, my ticket out of this splinter infested wood shack. I don't believe in ghosts, but I'll believe in anything if it means getting a good night's sleep. Why, for a well-rested night, I may even believe the Cubs could win the World Series.

Childhood Is... Telling Scary Stories.

Once upon a time...
STOP! I can't take it anymore!
8
kotecki
www.KimandJason.com © 2003 by Jason W. Kotecki

I don't think it's a tree...
I don't remember seeing any monster trees planted in the yard!

THE CHALKBOARD
What scared you the most as a kid?

"I was always scared of photos... I thought they would hurt... and absolutely refused to let photos be taken of me. I ripped out quite a large chunk of my mother's hair trying to escape the little black box once. And when I finally got a photo taken, I realized it didn't hurt but I was still scared of them hurting me, hence the many photos we have of my crying. "
Jo, age 20
Sydney, Australia

"I was really scared of owls. Pictures of them, as well as the ones in the woods behind our house!."
Chris, age 29
Madison, WI

"We had an outside toilet. To get to it you had to go out the back door, and then into the laundry. We also had a huge Gum Tree in our backyard. Everybody knows monsters hide behind Gum Trees - not to mention Drop Bears!!! I would open the back door very carefully at night, peer out, and then race into the laundry before the monsters had time to run from the tree to the door to catch me. And the procedure was repeated on the return to trip to the house..."
Anne, age 32
Thailand

"The scariest thing for me as a child was going down the cellar steps at my great aunt and uncle's house. It was creepy and dark, but the backs of the steps were open and I was deathly afraid that I would fall through them! I had to be carried down those steps many times to get root beer from my aunt's root beer box! Then, my father told me a monster lived down there under the steps in which made those steps even more scarier! Oh to be that frightful again! Those were the days!"
Sam Mylin, age 43
Willow Street, PA

THE GHOST PATROL

The sleepover ordeal led me to a perfect idea for a series of Halloween strips. Kim and Jason take their poltergeist problems into their own hands and form the Ghost Patrol. What results is kind of *Men in Black* meets *Ghostbusters,* but with a childlike spin. Of course, we also get some insightful commentary from Stinky and learn that Peter Venkman's proton pack has nothing on hairspray and a vacuum cleaner.

Our sleepover in the treehouse didn't last very long.
It's hard to sleep with ghosts flying everywhere.
Try sleeping with splinters in your bum, Mr. Warm And Fluffy Sleeping Bag!
www.KimandJason.com © 2003 by Jason W. Kotecki
kotecki

Stinky Speaks

I hope that's the last time I see the inside of that dank wood dungeon. The kids love it, but when you're used to the finer things in life, like heat sensitive foam neck support pillows and plush suede slippers, it can be a rough experience.

That's why I'd never make it on *Survivor.* I'd purposely stink up the entire cast just to get voted off first. Do they have bathtubs-full of tomato juice in the middle of nowhere?

I can't believe our night in the treehouse was ruined by ghosts.
I just wish there was something we could do about it.
We could call 911!
Yeah, and ask for a pizza, they'd like that.
www.KimandJason.com © 2003 by Jason W. Kotecki
kotecki

Stinky Speaks

I'm sure the good folks at 911 would be happy to help the kids with the ghosts that are haunting their treehouse.

They also enjoy answering Trivial Pursuit questions, helping with perplexing crossword puzzles, and looking for missing socks lost in the dryer.

TSSSHHH
Check THIS out!
What's with the hair-spray?
That ghost is stiff and can't move now!
How do you know a ghost is there?
Stinky told me.
I did?
Uh-oh. This isn't "extra hold".
www.KimandJason.com © 2003 by Jason W. Kotecki
kotecki

Stinky Speaks

Don't you just love it when people put words in your mouth? Of course, nobody seems to listen to what I'm actually saying...if they did, perhaps Kim wouldn't have just sprayed the banana bread her Mom set on the dining room table to cool...

VROOOOOMMMMM
So that's it? Freeze the ghost with hair spray and just suck him up with a vacuum?
Problem solved!
How'd you learn that?
Common sense, I guess.
So, what kind of batteries does this thing take?
www.KimandJason.com © 2003 by Jason W. Kotecki
kotecki

Stinky Speaks

Reminds me of the time she ran out of mayonnaise for her sandwich and used glue instead because it looked the same.

With Halloween so close, there's prob'ly tons of ghosts around.
Now that we can catch 'em, we should get rid of all the ghosts in the neighborhood.
Then people can pay us money, or candy or whatever.
I vote for candy. Cut out the middleman.
www.KimandJason.com © 2003 by Jason W. Kotecki
kotecki

Stinky Speaks

Typical kids; thinking not with their minds, but with their stomachs. Hey, what's a guy got to do to get a decent stuffed chicken marsala over here?

Childhood Is... Being A Candy Connoisseur.

© 2003 by Jason W. Kotecki
www.KimandJason.com
Hmm. Good peanut distribution. Nice, soft caramel, but way too much nougat.
Hey–I'll take your nougat! I love nougat!
Until someone explains to me EXACTLY what nougat is, I'll stick with Lady Godiva.
kotecki

Do you know why they call fall "fall"?
kotecki
Because of all the leaves that fall off the trees.
Oh.
Right.
Why, what did you think?
I thought it had to do with the World Serious or something.
www.KimandJason.com © 2003 by Jason W. Kotecki
Baseball?
Well, yeah! Aren't they always talking about fall balls and stuff?

Childhood Is... Leaf Piles.

Hey look! ANOTHER person raked up some leaves for us to jump into!
kotecki
www.KimandJason.com © 2003 by Jason W. Kotecki

Check us out, Boompa!
What do we have here?
www.KimandJason.com © 2003 by Jason W. Kotecki
I thought you were afraid of ghosts?
We're the GHOST PATROL!
Not anymore! We stop 'em cold with hairspray, and then vacuum 'em right up!
I'm impressed.
kotecki
Can you tell this is a clip-on?

The Ghost Patrol

Kim: This will be so great! We'll finally rid the world of all ghosts! No one will be scared ever again!

Jason: I still think people will be able to tell this is a clip-on...

So if I see any ghosts, all I need to do is call you and you'll take care of it?
At your service!
Do you have a card I can have?
www.KimandJason.com © 2003 by Jason W. Kotecki
Um, let me see...
kotecki
Here you go.
Mark Prior?
Don't worry. I have two.

The Ghost Patrol

Jason: I wonder why your Boompa asked for a card. I'm just happy I had one on me. Don't you think that's a little weird?

Kim: No. My Boompa does all kinds of weird things. You should see the weird shorts he wears when he cuts the grass.

I wonder if the people who invented hairspray ever thought it would be so good at freezing ghosts?
Prob'ly not. It's like one of those "happy accidents".
kotecki
www.KimandJason.com © 2003 by Jason W. Kotecki
Right. Like when Katie wipes out on her rollerblades.

The Ghost Patrol

Jason: I guess that would be considered a happy accident...

Kim: Of course it would! And so would the time that can of soda exploded right in her face. I know I was happy.

What the--?
TSSHHHH
kotecki
Don't worry, Katie!
We're just getting the ghosts out of your room.
www.KimandJason.com
Ghosts?! Get out of here!
© 2003 by Jason W. Kotecki
FOOMP!
MMMM
Oops. You've got more than one retainer, right?

The Ghost Patrol
Kim: You sucked up Katie's retainer? My Mom is not going to be happy to hear that.
Jason: Then she prob'ly won't like hearing how I accidentally sucked up a few of her earrings when we were in your parent's room.

kotecki
This thing's a pain!
It's hard to suck up ghosts lugging this around.
Here, try this.
The Ghost Patrol goes mobile?
www.KimandJason.com
© 2003 by Jason W. Kotecki
Yep. So let's get moving. I think my Mom saw me nab it from the closet.
VROOOMM

The Ghost Patrol
Kim: Man, this thing's powerful!
Jason: Not as powerful as the sound of my Mom yelling at me, so turn it down for now, will ya?

We're the Ghost Patrol!
We're here to exterminate your ghosts!
We work for candy.
Halloween is four days away! I don't have any candy yet!
1709
SLAM
kotecki
www.KimandJason.com
© 2003 by Jason W. Kotecki
We can work on credit!

The Ghost Patrol
Kim: That's the fourth guy who slammed his door on us.
Jason: Maybe we should put together some kind of early bird discount...

Hi. We're the Ghost Patrol. We work for --
OUT!
SLAM
That was quick.
We didn't even get to our jingle...
kotecki
www.KimandJason.com © 2003 by Jason W. Kotecki

The Ghost Patrol
Kim: Maybe we need some sort of commercial.
Jason: Well, we already have a good jingle. Now all we need is a famous celebrity or some babes.

If you hire us, we'll get rid of any ghosts you have.
www.KimandJason.com © 2003 by Jason W. Kotecki
You can pay us in candy.
Gaa!
kotecki
He's not our target market - plus he'll never pay.
You never know.
Trust me. When he does get his hands on candy, he doesn't even bother to take the wrapper off.

The Ghost Patrol
Jason: I've seen him eat an entire bag of jelly beans before.
Kim: Big whoop. I've done that.
Jason: No, I mean he ate the entire bag of jelly beans, price tag and all.

Boompa, have you seen any ghosts you need taken care of?
www.KimandJason.com © 2003 by Jason W. Kotecki
No, but here's some candy for your excellent service.
Wow - thanks!
Grandparents make the best customers!
They've had lots of practice.
kotecki

The Ghost Patrol
Jason: If we had more grandparents, we'd make a killing with this business.
Kim: Tell me about it. Even a dozen would be nice.

We're the Ghost Patrol.
We work for candy.
hair spray
vacuum
Oh, how cute!
www.KimandJason.com © 2003 by Jason W. Kotecki
VROOOM
TSSHHH
kotecki
Those ghosts are history! But she sure seemed surprised...
I don't blame her. She had a lot of them.

The Ghost Patrol

Jason: It was nice of that lady to give us all the candy. What a tip!

Kim: Yeah. Did you hear her saying something about "Help, help, go away"?

Jason: She was prob'ly yelling at the ghosts.

Childhood Is... Halloween: The Day After.

That was a lot of candy...I feel all shakey.
You look straight to me. Wanna split this King Size Snickers®?
kotecki

Hi. We're the Ghost Patrol.
We work for candy.
Halloween was last week! Go home!
www.KimandJason.com © 2003 by Jason W. Kotecki
SLAM!
kotecki
Looks like we're in a down market.

The Ghost Patrol

Jason: Looks like this market has dried up. I guess we've gotten rid of all the ghosts in this neighborhood.

Kim: Good. I'm almost out of hairspray. I've got to get this can back to Katie's room before she notices it's gone.

I hate how it gets dark so early these days.
I can barely fit in all the playing I need to do!
Did you know that when it's winter in Alaska, it's dark most of the day?
I bet the kids up there really get ripped on bedtimes.
kotecki

Dad, I've decided to start a new bedtime tax!
Oh yeah?
Yep. Every time I go to bed, I'd like a nickel.
Good, then I can stop paying you an allowance.
kotecki
www.KimandJason.com © 2003 by Jason W. Kotecki
Let's talk about my new tax cut plan...

ADDITIONAL REJECTED TAX PROPOSALS...

Bedtime Tax: 5¢
Clean Up My Bedroom Tax: 10¢
Wash The Dishes Tax: 10¢
Take Out The Garbage Tax: 25¢
Eat Onions Tax: $2.50

Well, Halloween is over. What's next?
Nothing 'till Christmas.
What about Thanksgiving?
Oh yeah. That's in there, too.
I **LOVE** Thanksgiving. Turkey, mashed potatoes, pumpkin pie...
It's just that you don't get any presents.
That would make me a **LOT** more thankful.
kotecki

Stinky, what do I have to do to get a dog?
Figure out how to make pigs fly?
I've been trying to keep my room clean lately.
So that's what it looks like when you're *trying?*
When will Mom and Dad see that I'm 'sponsible?
If only pigs had wings, you at least have a fighting chance.
www.KimandJason.com © 2003 by Jason W. Kotecki
kotecki

Stinky Speaks

I've seen some lost causes in my day, but this ranks right up there with the most hopeless. The kid killed her own goldfish when she took it out of the bowl to teach it tricks, for crying out loud!

Her parents have too much sense and too much compassion for innocent Golden Retrievers for them to cave and buy her a dog. And if she thinks her room is clean, well, I've seen teeming landfills with less clutter and mayhem than that disaster zone monstrosity she calls a bedroom.

Here's breakfast.
Cool! A smiley face.
www.KimandJason.com © 2003 by Jason W. Kotecki
Hey...tomorrow could you make it look more like The Rock?
kotecki

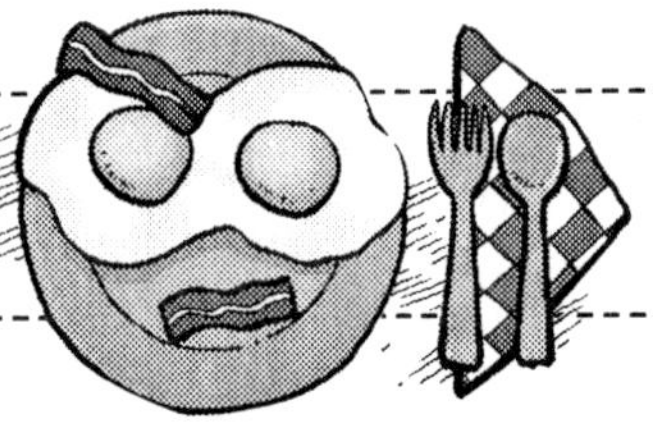

The peculiar thing about children is that they can turn any ordinary occurrence into a cause for great celebration.
kotecki
www.KimandJason.com © 2003 by Jason W. Kotecki
YES! My Mom put my Ace Laser sheets on my bed!
Rock on!
I rest my case.

Stinky Speaks

I once saw Kim go into uncontrollable convulsions of joy when she found out that her Mum was preparing mashed potatoes for dinner. I think I pulled something just watching her.

Childhood Is...
Being Just Like Dad.
Dad, I think your whip creme is spoiled.
www.KimandJason.com © 2003 by Jason W. Kotecki
kotecki

WHAT ON EARTH ARE YOU DOING!?
I tried to tell him, Mom.
Dougie, I TOLD you the grass should be green!
kotecki
www.KimandJason.com © 2003 by Jason W. Kotecki

I can't believe how lazy this squirrel is!
He's been sitting there all day and hasn't moved once.
Go find a nut or something!
Wanna go do some-thing?
No. I'm busy.
kotecki
www.KimandJason.com © 2003 by Jason W. Kotecki

Someday in the future, the world will be run by machines.
But who's gonna run the machines?
And what happens when the machines get bored, huh?
I'd say the Future's got its work cut out.
kotecki
www.KimandJason.com © 2003 by Jason W. Kotecki

Can I be excused?
No. You haven't even touched your food.
The meat looks a little fuzzy...
POKE
POKE
That's ridiculous.
I know! I didn't know meat could grow beards.
© 2003 by Jason W. Kotecki
www.KimandJason.com
kotecki

Mom, can I have some pop?
No.
But I'm THIRSTY.
Then have some water.
I'm not THAT kind of thirsty.
kotecki
www.KimandJason.com © 2003 by Jason W. Kotecki

thirsty: a poem by kim

all I want is some pop
but my mom said no way!
When I die of thirsty
then what will she say?

Mom, you know our doorknobs?
kotecki
You were pretty bored with those too, weren't you?
No...
Oh.
I see.
www.KimandJason.com © 2003 by Jason W. Kotecki
Any chance you could stay sitting there for about an hour?

Childhood Is...
Not Keeping Score.
Do we know who's winning?
No. But I have two home runs.
Kotecki
www.KimandJason.com © 2003 by Jason W. Kotecki

Do zoos go alligator shopping?
What?
Like when they need new animals, is there a store they go to?
kotecki
I think they catch 'em in the wild.
But they have pet stores where you can buy dogs or fish. It seems like there should be zoo stores.
Well there aren't.
But this is America! If I want a cheetah, I should be able to buy one!
Maybe Wal-Mart should work on that...
www.KimandJason.com © 2003 by Jason W. Kotecki

MOM! MOM! I think Dougie ate a marker cap!
WHAT?! What makes you think that?
kotecki
www.KimandJason.com © 2003 by Jason W. Kotecki
Well, I kinduv asked him to...
WHAT?!
But I didn't think he would!

If I was rich, a lot of things would be different in this world.
Like what?
Well for one, I'd have a lot more money.
www.KimandJason.com © 2003 by Jason W. Kotecki
kotecki

Katie, what's school like? Is it fun?
No. There's too much homework.
I can't wait to have homework!
If you were smarter, I'd have you do mine.
Then again, if you were smarter, you wouldn't have just said that.
www.KimandJason.com © 2003 by Jason W. Kotecki
kotecki

VRROOOO!
VROOO
WHAAA
WHAAA
Is that a kazoo?
Yep. Pretty good, huh?
Has your Mom heard you play?
Yep. Why do you think I'm out here?
www.KimandJason.com © 2003 by Jason W. Kotecki
kotecki

We've got 34 sleeps 'till Christmas.
That **MANY?!**
Boy, I wonder how old I'll be then...
TOYS
www.KimandJason.com © 2003 by Jason W. Kotecki
kotecki

Childhood Is...
Mom Washing Your Face.
Mom! You're gonna make it so I'll never need to shave!
kotecki

It's great to be alive. A miracle, actually.
kotecki
Trust me, it's certainly easy to take for granted.

THE PICKLES

A good deed by any other name is still a good deed. Some superheroes are called upon to save the world from nuclear holocaust; others are summoned to open a jar of pickles. A lot depends on whether or not you can fly, own a driver's license, or if you mom will let you out of the house.

I can't open this pickle jar!
kotecki
www.KimandJason.com © 2003 by Jason W. Kotecki
Here, you try.
I can't do it, but I know who can!
ZIP
Oh great.
I prefer "Super", but I'll take the compliment.

Super J's Super Secret Log #000025

I'm used to being complimented as a super hero. It goes with the territory. When most people see me, they almost always say something like, "Oh great," or "Here we go again," or "I can't believe you're here."

Get used to it folks. I'm here for the long haul. I won't abandon you.

What seems to be the problem, little fair-haired girl?
I told you–I can't open the pickle jar!
I see. You were wise to call me.
I didn't call you.
I could sense you were about to.
www.KimandJason.com © 2003 by Jason W. Kotecki
Kotecki
Can you open this or not?
And now I'm sensing impatience.

Super J's Super Secret Log #000026

One of my best powers is my ability to sense things. I have super sensing abilities. Kind of like Spiderman except without the spider part.

I can sense trouble from any distance. I can sense when there are damsels in the stress. Right now, I can sense that you're reading. Pretty good, huh?

Stand back and allow Super J to open this pickle jar.
You're no help at all!
Funny, this label doesn't even *MENTION* Kryptonite.
kotecki
www.KimandJason.com © 2003 by Jason W. Kotecki

Super J's Super Secret Log #000027

This pickle jar is a surprisingly strong foe. So strong that the only reason I can't open it must be because it contains Kryptonite somehow. But where? Perhaps that mysterious green liquid is Kryptonite juice. I don't know, but I have a hunch that "Vlasic" might mean Kryptonite in some other mysterious language...like Spanish or something.

I'll just ask my Dad to open the jar.
NONSENSE!
No job is too hard for Super J!
CURSE YOU, PICKLE JAR! CURSE YOU!
kotecki
www.KimandJason.com © 2003 by Jason W. Kotecki

Super J's Super Secret Log #000028

I don't usually lose my composure like this. This thing must be glued on. With super glue. And nailed shut.

You may think I'm discouraged and defeated. I'm not. I'm just trying to act that way so the pickle jar will be fooled and release his hold.

And if that doesn't work, I'll have to find Jason's Dad's hammer.

Super J is more persistent than pickles!

This pickle jar has been a formidable foe...
But Super J is more persistent than pickles!
Uh-oh.
CRASH
Great. I'm dead.
Pickle?
kotecki
www.KimandJason.com © 2003 by Jason W. Kotecki

Super J's Super Secret Log #000029

Ah-ha! Mission accomplished! Pickles abound!

No one ever said crime-fighting was easy - or clean! Now, I must quickly go save the day for someone else, for evil lurks elsewhere, far away from the approaching footsteps of the little fair-haired girl's Mom!

Childhood Is... Mysterious Accidents.

How did this pickle jar break?
Perhaps it hit the floor with great force?
kotecki
www.KimandJason.com © 2003 by Jason W. Kotecki

Well, I'm going to bed...
WHAT?! We haven't even had lunch.
I know. Wake me up in 24 days, please.
24 DAYS!?
That's right. There's no way I can last 'till Christmas.
So I'm just going to sleep right now, and when I wake up, Christmas will be here.
Don't forget to wake me - I don't want to miss it.
YAWN! What day is it? I must have really been out of it!
It's still today.
Shoot.
www.KimandJason.com © 2003 by Jason W. Kotecki
kotecki

Want to help us decorate the Christmas tree?
Sure!
Great! I'll be right over-bye!
I thought we were helping decorate your tree?
You are. My Dad is putting on the lights.
It's much safer over here.
Especially since I didn't quite check all the lights...
www.KimandJason.com
© 2003 by Jason W. Kotecki
kotecki

TRUE STORY. The safest place to be when my Dad was putting on the Christmas tree lights was anywhere but in the house. Learning to ride a unicycle on a busy interstate would be safer. All seriousness aside, I loved putting the ornaments on the tree. Maybe it was because of the huge build-up of suspense. It took my Dad the better part of a Saturday to cram them all on there. And when I say cram, I mean it. I don't know if he was trying to outdo Clark W. Griswold from *Christmas Vacation* fame, or if he had a personal vendetta against the electric company, but the thing looked very much like it was on fire by the time he was done. I believe he and my Mom have a pre-lit tree now, which is good for everyone, but I know I'll miss seeing that special wonder of the world - a tree with more lights than needles. -- Jason

I'm asking Santa for two ponies this year.
TWO?
He'll prob'ly think two is too much, so he'll just get me one, which is what I really want.
I don't think it's a good idea to trick Santa.
Fine.
I'll erase the part about being sixteen.
kotecki
www.KimandJason.com © 2003 by Jason W. Kotecki

Did you write a Christmas list for Santa?
Yeah! Wanna see it?
I can barely read it.
I think it's been through the wash a few times.
It's been in my pocket since July.
kotecki
www.KimandJason.com © 2003 by Jason W. Kotecki

How picky do you think Santa is when deciding how good you've been?
I hope he doesn't hold the "Burning Slipper" incident against me!
It's hard to be good for a whole year!
Hey, I'm the one who's always said we need more Christmases.
kotecki
www.KimandJason.com © 2003 by Jason W. Kotecki

I've decided not to ask for the swing set this year.
No?
I think it might ruin my chances of getting the roller coaster.
Good point.
Besides, it's not like the x-ray machine is a shoo-in.
kotecki
www.KimandJason.com © 2003 by Jason W. Kotecki

"Santa smelled like cole slaw..."

Childhood Is... Your Favorite Christmas Ornament.

Mom, how come I don't see my ornament on here?
That's **real** gold paint I used on that macaroni!
Kotecki
www.KimandJason.com © 2003 by Jason W. Kotecki

Happy Holidays
Why are you so scared of that mall Santa? You ruined the picture **AGAIN!**
He smelled like cole slaw...
Kotecki
www.KimandJason.com © 2003 by Jason W. Kotecki

THE ELF JOB

Ever wonder where Santa gets his elves? What are his hiring practices? What does he look for in his employees? Are the pointy ears a prerequisite? In this episode, Kim and Jason explore these questions and more. Every Christmas season, I look for a unique story angle. This gets more and more challenging with each passing year. I think this one was pretty original; it sure was fun to write.

I thought you already mailed your list to Santa.
I did. This is a job application.
I'm applying for a job as an elf!
At the North Pole?
Yep. How do you spell 401 k?
kotecki

I didn't know Santa was hiring elves.
Everybody needs help during the holidays.
But you're not even an ELF!
But I'm SHORT!
www.KimandJason.com © 2003 by Jason W. Kotecki
Well, let's all hope Santa is equal opportunity.
kotecki

You're still working on that job application?
I want to make it so Santa would be CRAZY to not hire me.
"Expert Toy Tester"? "Professional Play Advisor"?
Too much? I don't want to sound over-qualified...
www.KimandJason.com © 2003 by Jason W. Kotecki
kotecki

Mom, does this need more stamps?
What? Why?
www.KimandJason.com © 2003 by Jason W. Kotecki
I'm mailing a job application to the North Pole.
I'm gonna be an elf!
Why don't you let me take care of that...
You know where Santa lives?
I'll make sure he gets it.
GREAT!
Can I get a tracking number?
kotecki
Any word back from Santa on my elf job application?
Jason, I just mailed it this morning.
www.KimandJason.com © 2003 by Jason W. Kotecki
Oh.
Right.
I'll check back after cartoons.
kotecki
My job application to the North Pole has been mailed out!
It's only a matter of time before I'm an OFFICIAL elf!
How do you think Santa will let you know? A phone call? Or maybe a letter?
kotecki
www.KimandJason.com © 2003 by Jason W. Kotecki
I figured he'd have some sort of press conference.
Do you have any questions you want me to ask the big guy?
The BIG GUY?
www.KimandJason.com © 2003 by Jason W. Kotecki
Yeah, Santa! For when he hires me to be an elf.
You already have nicknames for him? He hasn't even hired you!
kotecki
I just want to fit in. Now how do you feel about S-Dog?

Childhood Is... Decorating Cookies.

You better tell your Mom we'll need more frosting.
© 2003 by Jason W. Kotecki
www.KimandJason.com
kotecki

Boompa, did Santa come to your house when you were little?
Yep.
So he's been doing that job a long time...
He has been around awhile.
Do you KNOW him?
You could say that...
Do you think you could tell him not to retire 'till after I get big?
www.KimandJason.com © 2003 by Jason W. Kotecki
kotecki

Are you PACKING?
I want to be ready when Santa hires me to be an elf.
I wonder if he'll have the reindeers pick me up!
I'm just not sure if you're elf material.
Fine. I see SOMEONE who won't be petting Prancer.
© 2003 by Jason W. Kotecki
www.KimandJason.com
kotecki

Mom, is the mail running today?
Yes.
Are the phone lines down?
No.
Have aliens sabotoged the Earth's satellites?
Of course not.
Weird. I wonder why I haven't heard from Santa about my job application...
© 2003 by Jason W. Kotecki
kotecki
www.KimandJason.com

No word from the North Pole on that elf job, huh?
Nothing yet.
I'm beginning to suspect a clerical error.
Or maybe someone in Santa's office messed up.
kotecki
www.KimandJason.com
© 2003 by Jason W. Kotecki

What's the matter?
I haven't heard back from Santa about my job application.
Why wouldn't he want me for an elf?
Maybe he doesn't think I'm good enough.
I think you're good enough.
I should've padded my resume more.
kotecki
www.KimandJason.com
© 2003 by Jason W. Kotecki

IT CAME!
A letter back from Santa about my job application!
Read it! What does it say?
Dear Jason, we got your application here at the North Pole. I'd like to hire you as an elf, but elves aren't allowed to get gifts. If we hired you, I wouldn't know what to do with all your presents.
Merry Christmas,
Santa
Disappointed?
Well, I'd hate to have good presents go to waste.
kotecki
www.KimandJason.com
© 2003 by Jason W. Kotecki

Childhood Is... Unbridled Anticipation.

Is it Christmas YET?
NOW
When will it be here?
NOW?
NOW.
Is it today?
TOMORROW?
Why not?
When?
Is it almost here?
How much longer?
How about tomorrow?
How 'bout now?
How long 'till Christmas?
Are you SURE?
Is it NOW?
How about NO
OW?
Kotecki

Looks like we're almost out of fruit punch!
Don't worry. I'm almost done.
How do you spell "spectacular"?
Kotecki

JASON
Kotecki
www.KimandJason.com © 2003 by Jason W. Kotecki

CHRISTMAS CAROL Match Game
• WE THREE KINGS
• LET IT SNOW
• JINGLE BELL ROCK
• RUDOLPH THE RED-NOSED REINDEER
Kotecki

Happy birthday, little guy!
Want me to blow out your candle for you?
Kotecki www.KimandJason.com © 2003 by Jason W. Kotecki

Did Santa eat all the milk and cookies you left out?
Yep! But I had my Dad make him a milk shake instead.
© 2003 by Jason W. Kotecki
Kotecki
www.KimandJason.com
You know, something different.
That was awfully nice of your Dad.
He didn't seem to mind. He made it pretty big, too.

Childhood Is... Getting Tired Out From Playing With New Christmas Toys.

kotecki
www.KimandJason.com © 2003 by Jason W. Kotecki

What are you doing?
I'm waiting for this hot dog to turn blue.
kotecki
Katie said hot dogs turn blue if you microwave them for five minutes!
www.KimandJason.com © 2003 by Jason W. Kotecki
BLAM
Hey– it's not BLUE!
I thought you said you put a hot dog in there...

Do you think chickens can play checkers?
It's pretty easy to play...
Prob'ly not. They don't really have hands.
That's too bad.
kotecki
www.KimandJason.com © 2003 by Jason W. Kotecki
Chickens. They can lay eggs, but they can't even play checkers.

Happy New Year's Eve!
Just like Christmas Eve, but without the presents.
kotecki
Do you have any New Year's revolutions?
Yep!
www.KimandJason.com © 2003 by Jason W. Kotecki
I revolve to eat more chocolate!

Why do people make such a big deal about New Year's Day?
www.KimandJason.com © 2004 by Jason W. Kotecki
It's a fresh start. A new beginning. A clean slate.
Isn't every day like that?
What's so big about THIS one?
Maybe it has a better agent.
kotecki

Have you ever had liver tea?
www.KimandJason.com © 2004 by Jason W. Kotecki
GROSS! No Way!
Me neither. I don't know ANYONE who has!
So?
What made that guy who wrote the pledge decide it would be good to promise liver tea and justice for all?
kotecki

Do you think real angels make snow angels?
They prob'ly make snow humans.
But in the clouds instead of the snow.
kotecki
www.KimandJason.com © 2004 by Jason W. Kotecki
Yeah. They prob'ly hate getting snow up their sheet.

THE COLD

Being sick is no fun. But that doesn't mean it can't be funny.

Mom, I don't feel too good.
Hmm. You feel warm.
You must have a cold.
Now how does that make sense?
www.KimandJason.com © 2004 by Jason W. Kotecki

Jason's sick.
So I hear.
I'm bored.
It's no fun playing checkers alone.
I keep losing to myself.
www.KimandJason.com © 2004 by Jason W. Kotecki

"I keep losing to myself."

What's that?
It's my will. In case I don't pull through.
I don't think that's necessary.
I'm just supposed to trust what you and Dad will do with all 147 of my Star Warriors guys?
I don't think so, Mom.
www.KimandJason.com © 2004 by Jason W. Kotecki

“Goodbye forever, moon vacation.”

Mom, could you call that place that gives wishes to kids that are sick?
I've got my **PERFECT** wish.
You have a cold. I doubt you qualify.
Goodbye forever, moon vacation.
www.KimandJason.com © 2004 by Jason W. Kotecki
Kotecki

Kotecki
PBBTFFTP
I made some chicken soup to make you feel better.
Moms are the only good thing about being sick.
www.KimandJason.com © 2004 by Jason W. Kotecki

Childhood Is... Cold Medicine.

© 2004 by Jason W. Kotecki
www.KimandJason.com
POISONED- by my own Mom!
I can see you're feeling better already.
Kotecki

You're sick. You're not supposed to be outside.
I'm not. I'm in my room. Are you gonna throw me a snowball or not?
kotecki
www.KimandJason.com © 2004 by Jason W. Kotecki

Childhood Is... The Lost Mitten.

Where **IS** that stupid thing?!
kotecki
www.KimandJason.com © 2004 by Jason W. Kotecki

Childhood Is...
Ketchup On Everything.
Are those green beans?
Yeah.
So?
kotecki
www.KimandJason.com © 2004 by Jason W. Kotecki

THE SNOWFORT

In every good story, there has to be an effective antagonist. When it comes to childhood, I've found that older siblings can fill that role quite well. (At least that's what I've been told – I'm the oldest of three boys.) Katie is the quintessential evil older sister, and a constant source of irritation for Kim and Jason. I particularly enjoyed writing Kim's poems that were featured on the website. Someday, I'd like to write a children's book in a similar format. That could be fun.

Wanna see my snowfort?
It's in-destructable!
Sure!
www.KimandJason.com © 2004 by Jason W. Kotecki
Oh great!
The family minivan: grocery getter AND weapon of mass destruction.
Kotecki

snowfort: a poem by kim

i bilt a big snowfort
akording to plan
but now it is toast
thanks to our van

From our super-secure fort, we'll be able to attack our fiercest enemies!
Kotecki
Nice ant hill, losers.
www.KimandJason.com © 2004 by Jason W. Kotecki
With big sisters like her, who needs enemies?

bigger: a poem by kim

My sister is mean
but what can I do?
She's bigger than me
and uglier too.

Our ammunition is all ready!
We'll NEVER run out!
Here, this one's got Katie's name all over it!
kotecki
www.KimandJason.com © 2004 by Jason W. Kotecki
Where...?

melted: a poem by kim

This ones for Katie her name mustuv melted
it wont matter at all onse shes been pelted!

There she is!
It's KATIE!
GET HER!
kotecki
www.KimandJason.com © 2004 by Jason W. Kotecki
PLOP
SHOOT! We built the snowfort too far away!

missed: a poem by kim

I tried to nail Katie too bad i missed
now my hole life will sees to egsist!

Were you trying to hit me with this snowball?
No...I, uh... thought you'd like to play catch...
What are all these for?
Lots of catch?
www.KimandJason.com © 2004 by Jason W. Kotecki
I don't think she bought it.
I don't think I can feel my face...
kotecki

liver: a poem by kim

I can't feel my face or even my liver
i think i can feel my spleen start to shiver.

Childhood Is... Visions of Snowfort Grandiosity.

Let's get the elevator done first. Then we can ask your Boompa if he has scaffolding.
Kotecki
www.KimandJason.com © 2004 by Jason W. Kotecki

More snow?
No, more mountains.
Kotecki
www.KimandJason.com © 2004 by Jason W. Kotecki

Childhood Is...
Snowball Preservation.
We'll put it in here...
Then in July, we'll give Katie the surprise of her life!
Kotecki
www.KimandJason.com © 2004 by Jason W. Kotecki

THE SUPER BOWL COMMERCIAL

Kim and Jason have had some fun in the past with Kim's dad's video camera. (A little too much fun perhaps, considering it was pretty much obliterated during a hunt for tornados.) Well, Dad got a new camera, and the kids came up with a new way to use (abuse?) it. What resulted is a look at Super Bowl marketing hooplah through the eyes of children. Happily, no video cameras were harmed in the making of *this* episode.

I guess the Super Bowl is only a few weeks away.
Will that Lavron James guy be playing?
No, silly, he's a basketball player.
Well, how am I supposed to know?
For crying out loud, it's not like I follow baseball or anything.
© 2004 by Jason W. Kotecki
www.KimandJason.com
kotecki

BEHIND THE SCENES

The Making of a Super Bowl Commercial

Kim: I really don't know that much about Super Bowls or baseball, but I do know a lot about commercials.
Jason: You do?
Kim: Yes, remember, we did that infomercial about grilled cheese? That was some of my best work. And your Mom's grilled cheeses were not too shabby, either.
Jason: By the way, it's LeBron James.
Kim: No, I'm pretty sure you're Mom made them.

The only thing I like about the Super Bowl is the commercials.
That's the best part.
They're always so funny!
Yes, nothing says pinnacle of western humor like talking sock puppets and animated beer bottles.
© 2004 by Jason W. Kotecki
www.KimandJason.com
kotecki

BEHIND THE SCENES

The Making of a Super Bowl Commercial

Kim: My favorite commercial is that one with the guy who talks about that thing and then at the end, he gets hit by that other thing.
Jason: I don't remember that one. Do you remember what it was a commercial for?
Kim: I don't know. Something.

Let's make our **OWN** Super Bowl commercial!
Whose camera is that?
My Dad's.
I thought you broke it when we went storm chasing?
I did. This is new.
Will he be mad that we're using it?
No.
Well, only if he finds out.
www.KimandJason.com © 2004 by Jason W. Kotecki
kotecki

BEHIND THE SCENES

The Making of a Super Bowl Commercial

Jason: The main thing you need when you want to make a Super Bowl commercial is a camera.
Kim: The video kind.
Jason: It's a good thing that Kim was able to borrow her Dad's camera.
Kim: Yeah, my Dad's cool about it. I've found that as long as I put it back where I found it before he knows it's gone, I really don't need to ask him about it.

Mom, I need to borrow some noodles.
What for?
We're filming a Super Bowl commercial.
Really.
Okay. Knock yourself out.
Hey, do you think--
Don't push your luck.
www.KimandJason.com © 2004 by Jason W. Kotecki
kotecki

BEHIND THE SCENES

The Making of a Super Bowl Commercial

Jason: So we decided to use noodles as the product to advertise for our Super Bowl commercial. Mostly because Kim likes noodles, and mostly because I'm not sure how to make soda cans look like they're talking and playing football.
Kim: I can't believe your Mom let you have the box of noodles.
Jason: I know. I should've asked for the fire extinguisher first.

"I'm always in favor of explosions."

Super Bowl commercial about noodles-
take one!
www.KimandJason.com © 2004 by Jason W. Kotecki
This seems a little boring.
I'm always in favor of explosions.
To the microwave!
kotecki

Jason: So the microwave thing didn't work too well.
Kim: For the noodles OR the microwave.
Jason: We got some great footage though.
Kim: I'll say. I never knew microwaves could jump.

BEHIND THE SCENES

The Making of a Super Bowl Commercial

Life has its share of twists and turns.
It seems like just yesterday when I was up for a role opposite Tom Hanks in Cast Away.
Long story short, I didn't get the part.
Now here I am filming imaginary Super Bowl commercials.
Can we get him to look more "macho"?
I HATE that stupid volleyball...
www.KimandJason.com © 2004 by Jason W. Kotecki
kotecki

KIM & JASON SUPER BOWL COMMERCIAL: OUTTAKES

Silly skunk, noodles are for kids!
They're GRREAT!
kotecki
Noodles. The breakfast of champions.
www.KimandJason.com © 2004 by Jason W. Kotecki
Hey, do you have a pirate hat?
CAP'N CRUNCH

BEHIND THE SCENES

Jason: We ended up doing quite a few takes for our commercial. We thought of some of our favorite cereal commercials, and we suddenly had some really good ideas.
Kim: I sure wish we had the phone number of those Rice Krispies dudes. They make good commercials. They sure are funny. And good actors.

plain noodles 14 cents.
cheese 18 hundrid fiftee.
cheese and noodles together priceliss
www.KimandJason.com © 2004 by Jason W. Kotecki
CUT! I think we spelled "cheese" wrong...
cheese and noodles together priceliss
kotecki

BEHIND THE SCENES

Jason: I'm pretty sure we spelled "cheese" right, but doesn't noodles have three "o's"?
Kim: Who knows...
Jason: We could prob'ly look it up in the dictionary.
Kim: How can we do that if we don't know how it's spelled?

I used to really like basghetti. I ate it all the time.
Then I tried macaroni. It's more fun to eat. It's just better.
www.noodles.com/switch
www.KimandJason.com © 2004 by Jason W. Kotecki
I'm Kim. And I'm a switcher.
kotecki

BEHIND THE SCENES

Kim: I still like basghetti, don't get me wrong. But with macaroni, those little guys just make my mouth happier. Those bow tie dudes are prob'ly my favorite, but your Mom gave us a box of macaroni, not the bow ties.
Jason: Yeah, sometimes you just have to make do with what you've got. You're Boompa says that.
Kim: No, he says, "You've got to make dude with what you've got."

Wanna watch a Super Bowl commercial. Boompa?
But the game's not 'till Sunday.
We filmed this one ourselves!
It's about NOODLES!
Hmmm, this should be good.
It is! Even without the pyrotechnics.
kotecki
www.KimandJason.com © 2004 by Jason W. Kotecki

BEHIND THE SCENES

Jason: It's always exciting when you show your commercial to someone for the first time. I mean, we put a lot of work into this thing.

Kim: It's like they say, "It's a lavor of love." I'm not sure what that means, except something about love. And we sure love it.

It's all set to go!
What is?
Our Super Bowl commercial! Once the game comes on, I'll push play, and millions of people will see it!
That's not how VCRs work, morons.
Katie, we KNOW how it works.
Next thing you know, she'll be poking holes in our plan to sell it on Pay-Per-View.
kotecki
www.KimandJason.com © 2004 by Jason W. Kotecki

BEHIND THE SCENES

Jason: Your sister can't help but get her big fat nose into our business, can she?

Kim: She's just jealous of all the money we'll make on Pay-Per-View. And that all of her friends at school will be like, "Hey, aren't you Kim's sister? The one who made that really cool Super Bowl commercial?"

Jason: Right!

Kim: When we put this tape in and people watch our commercial, nobody will even remember who is playing in the game, or who has the most home runs!

The Super Bowl attracts one of the largest television audiences all year.
And with an audience THAT big, it's only natural for everyone to have their own perspective.
That boy playing quarterback is cute.
Now, why do they have to dance every time they make a tackle?
My aunt knows you're running off tackle! Would play-action kill you?
Wait, I thought you were supposed to dribble when you run...
Ask your Boompa if he's gonna order the pizza soon.
Kotecki

THE CARPENTER'S APPRENTICE

Kim used to spend a lot of time following her dad and Boompa as they worked on various projects. From what I hear, she was very "helpful." I often wonder what the exchanges sounded like. This episode tries to capture the spirit of a little girl who looks up to her grandfather...a little girl who wants nothing more than to be of valuable help...a little girl who is very, very aggressive with sandpaper.

Whatcha workin' on, Boompa?
Some shelves for your Mom.
Can I watch?
Sure.
So, when do we pull out the power tools?
www.KimandJason.com © 2004 by Jason W. Kotecki
kotecki

"I remember when I was a kid watching my grandfather fashion rocking chairs out of knotty pine wood. I always wanted to help him, too. Of course, there were no power tools back then. Although if there were, I'd dare say that I'd be quite taken by them myself. I remember that all the tools seemed so old, as if they'd been used a million times to build a million different things. And my grandfather, he seemed old too, at least to my young eyes. Now I see why he didn't mind me pestering him; I helped keep him young." -- Boompa

Boompa, you've got sawdust all over the floor!
Sometimes, do you sweep it all together and make sawdust angels?
No, I can't say that I have...
I definitely think it would be a lot easier to make them if you DID sweep it together.
www.KimandJason.com © 2004 by Jason W. Kotecki
kotecki

"You learn something new everyday, I guess. I've never tried it, but I reckon it would be much easier to create a sawdust angel when all the sawdust is swept together in one pile. I can't wait to hear what she thinks should be done with those saw horses." -- Boompa

"So when do we pull out the power tools?"

Boompa, can I help?
Can you be safe?
I know **all about** safety! I'll be right back!
See, I'm safe!
Very good.
Do you think I'll need a hard hat?

"I don't believe I've seen a better potential safety spokesgirl than this granddaughter of mine. Or a better idea of what it might be like to cross Betty Crocker with Johnny Bench." -- Boompa

Here Kim, you can help me sand this.
OK!
You probably won't need the oven mitts. Here's some sandpaper.
Sandpaper?
I bet this must come from trees that grow on beaches!

"If you can think of a better explanation of where sandpaper comes from, I'd sure like to hear it." -- Boompa

It's weird how sandpaper that's rough can make wood so smooth.
That's how life can be.
Sometimes things seem a lot smoother after we've been through rough times.
I guess. But who wants to be rubbed by sandpaper?

"Every once in a while I try to pass a little wisdom on to the next generation. Most of the time I do that, I'm reminded of how little I really know." -- Boompa

Childhood IS...
Being Grandpa's Assistant.
www.KimandJason.com © 2004 by Jason W. Kotecki
How's the sanding coming?
I'm almost done!

What's THIS called?
Why do you have two of these?
Boy, this sure is heavy!
What's THIS for?
I like helping you, Boompa!
What would you do without me?
It's hard to imagine.
Kotecki
www.KimandJason.com © 2004 by Jason W. Kotecki

Whoever invented the napkin was an amateur.
You don't like napkins?
They're just so one-dimensional.
Now the guy who invented sleeves...
GENIUS!
www.KimandJason.com © 2004 by Jason W. Kotecki
kotecki

Come on! We need to get out of here.
If there's one thing in life I've learned...
It's that big sisters are touchy about their things.
Why? What's going on?
Unless you can put lava back in its lamp, I'll tell you at your house.
www.KimandJason.com © 2004 by Jason W. Kotecki

Mom, I think I need new shoes.
Why, do they not fit?
Well, they certainly don't fit the image I'm trying to project.
My Mom sure knows how to waste good advertising dollars.
www.KimandJason.com © 2004 by Jason W. Kotecki
kotecki

Will these batteries work?
I don't know. What do they say?
Well, they have a "plus" and a "minus" on them.
Wait, these must be calculator batteries.
That's okay. My Dad has some in his alarm clock!
www.KimandJason.com © 2004 by Jason W. Kotecki
kotecki

Who decided you have to be sixteen to drive?
Why not fifteen? Why not **FIVE?**
What could I possibly know then that I don't know now?
It's prob'ly dangerous to drive if you can't see over the steering wheel.
What, do cars suddenly not have seat-belts and airbags?
Kotecki
www.KimandJason.com © 2004 by Jason W. Kotecki

Childhood IS...
Candy Hearts.
TRUE LOVE
BE MINE
www.KimandJason.com © 2004 by Jason W. Kotecki
"UR Special". Ha! These are like that Lucky Charms© cereal, but with words.
Hey, good thinking! We'll need the milk.
Kotecki

SPIT
All clean!
Kotecki
www.KimandJason.com © 2004 by Jason W. Kotecki

THE OUT-OF-WORK SUPERHERO

If anyone ever tells you that being a superhero is always glamorous and that superheroes are always adored by the people they protect, well, Super J would probably like to know their secret.

Hi little girl! Would you like me to do something **SUPER** for you?
No.
How about an autograph to make your friends jealous?
No.
Balloon animal?
Superheroes shouldn't have to work so hard to drum up business.
kot≡cki
www.KimandJason.com © 2004 by Jason W. Kotecki

Super J's Super Secret Log #000030

It's been a slow week being a superhero. It always seems like Superman and Batman and Spiderman are always busy fighting off the bad guys. I don't remember them offering to create balloon animals for their fans.

But I bet I could make a better one than Superman.

Way better.

If you're a superhero, how come I don't notice any super powers?
kot≡cki
WHAT? What about my 3-D vision? And how I can run **REALLY** fast?
Can you fly? Can you shoot webs?
No...
See?
www.KimandJason.com © 2004 by Jason W. Kotecki
HEY-BATMAN CAN'T FLY! SUPERMAN CAN'T SHOOT WEBS!

Super J's Super Secret Log #000031

I can't believe how hard it is to impress people these days. They've seen everything. I'd like her to tell The Flash that running really fast isn't a super power. I wonder if he has these problems...heck, his uniform isn't even that cool.

At least I have a cape. And capes used to mean something.

Hey. Kim's Boompa?
Yes, Jason.
It's Super J, actually.
Oh yes, right.
www.KimandJason.com © 2004 by Jason W. Kotecki
Are superheroes sometimes unappreciated by regular people?
I suppose sometimes people have trouble seeing the greatness in others.
I knew it.
I'm before my time.
kotecki

Super J's Super Secret Log #000032

Now it all makes sense to me. I'm a prodigy, a freak of nature, a superhero from the future. I'm way ahead of my time and people don't understand me. Regular people who don't have super powers like I do have a hard time understanding me. It's not their fault. They're just not capable of comprehending all of my powers.

I guess that's why my Mom wastes my time by making me take out the garbage all the time.

I'm off on another dangerous mission.
Oh yeah? Like what?
I wouldn't want to frighten you with the details.
Wait. Does this have something to do with all of the snowballs on the front porch?
kotecki
www.KimandJason.com © 2004 by Jason W. Kotecki
If you mean frozen death spheres, I know not what you speak of.

Super J's Super Secret Log #000033

After the little fair-haired girl's mysterious probing questions, I rushed back outside to check the frozen death spheres to see if any were missing. Sure enough, after I counted them up, I'm pretty sure one or two were stolen.

Unfortunately, I can't be sure, because I forgot to count them after I made, er, discovered them.

I see your friend is wearing his underpants on the outside of his jeans again.
Yes, it's his uniform.
He thinks he's a superhero.
Kotecki
www.KimandJason.com © 2004 by Jason W. Kotecki
Is that supposed to explain why he's outside without a coat throwing snowballs at the mailman?

Super J's Super Secret Log #000034

The mailman looked suspicious. I had to act fast, there was no time for drawn out questioning. I trusted my super senses and began hurling the frozen death spheres at him. The surprise attack worked perfectly; the sinister alien in disguise didn't even know what hit him. One death sphere nailed him right in the nose, the other clobbered him in the ear. I think I knocked him unconscious. I checked his "mailbag" for clues. I found a bunch of letters addressed to people I've never heard of, and a few *Pottery Barn* magazines. Very interesting.

I'm not sure what it all means, but rest assured, I WILL get to the bottom of this.

Childhood is...
Moms Ruining Everything.
Don't forget your coat!
Kotecki
www.KimandJason.com © 2004 by Jason W. Kotecki

Super J's Super Secret Log #000035

What are the bad guys going to think if I show that I'm affected by the elements? I've never seen Spiderman in furry earmuffs or Superman with stupid mittens.

Thanks a lot, Mom. Now no one will take me serious.

Hey, is that supposed to be you?
No, little fair-haired girl! Don't be seduced by his LIES!
He's taken on a form to make you think he's ME!
He's an alien sent from Xarnon to destroy me!
But don't be fooled! He's an IMPOSTER!
Whatever.
Good for you! Resist his power!
RESIST!
Kotecki
www.KimandJason.com
© 2004 by Jason W. Kotecki

www.KimandJason.com © 2004 by Jason W. Kotecki
Kotecki
Jason, quit playing with your food.
Oh, it's okay. I wasn't planning on eating it.

Tomorrow is going to be a great day!
What about today?
www.KimandJason.com © 2004 by Jason W. Kotecki
No. Today already blew it.
Kotecki

What's THAT?
Chicken noodle soup.
Are those sprinkles?
I like to add my own "extras": raisins, Froot Loops,® chocolate chips...
Do you always eat it like that?
Oh no.
But we were all out of marshmallows today.
www.KimandJason.com © 2004 by Jason W. Kotecki
Kotecki

Phone Book
HELLO PAGES
God must have written the phone book.
Why do you think that?
Because I can't think of anybody else who knows EVERYBODY!
www.KimandJason.com © 2004 by Jason W. Kotecki
Kotecki

Jason, do you know how this bowl got chipped?
I refuse to say anything without my lawyer present.
I wish I lived on TV.
www.KimandJason.com © 2004 by Jason W. Kotecki
Kotecki

Childhood is...
Reading Animal Books.
Did you know birds don't have lips?
Must be tricky for the girl birds to put on lipstick.
www.KimandJason.com © 2004 by Jason W. Kotecki
Kotecki

HEY! You're just in time!
For what?
To watch me hurl this giant snowball into outer space!
All I need to do now is build the catapult.
www.KimandJason.com © 2004 by Jason W. Kotecki
kotecki

THE GROCERY STORE

I always loved going to the grocery store with my mom. Somehow, I always got the feeling that she didn't share this feeling with me. Was it the constant fighting with my brother over who got to stand on the front of the cart? Was it the occasional pestering for a box of animal crackers? This little episode is my way of saying, "That's okay, Mom. I get it now."

Kim, get your coat. We're going to the grocery store.
© 2004 by Jason W. Kotecki
Can I bring Stinky?
I don't care.
KimandJason.com
C'mon, Stinky! We might get free samples!
As if they could CHARGE for those hot dogs with cheese in them...
kotecki

Stinky Speaks

Personally, I look forward to the day I go into a supermarket and get to feast on samples of prime rib, grilled and seasoned to perfection. And not microscopic size samples that leave you tasting more air than anything.

Obviously, that day isn't coming anytime soon. Unless, perhaps, the public rises up and revolts against the over-processed meat stand-ins stuffed with something that resembles cheese in color only, if cheese was normally the color orange the transportation department uses on cautionary signs to keep us from hurting ourselves and others.

Maybe we need a few of those signs stationed near the free sample lady, eh?

Are we almost there yet?
Almost.
kotecki
www.KimandJason.com © 2004 by Jason W. Kotecki
Oh dear, here we go...
THE NOODLE AISLE!
Somewhere, someone named Atkins shudders.
Mom, shouldn't we get another cart?

Stinky Speaks

I've never seen anyone with such an insatiable appetite for noodles than Kim. It's unbelievable. If left to her own desires, she'd probably eat more noodles than the population of Sicily over the course of a year. I guess there are worse addictions in this world. I certainly have my own vices.

I wouldn't wish the craving of high-end French pastries on anyone's waistline.

These days, the size of product packaging borders on ridiculous.
I was unaware of the huge public demand for mayonnaise in five-gallon drums.
www.KimandJason.com © 2004 by Jason W. Kotecki
Look Mom! ULTRA SIZE!
SOAPY SOAP
And that we all desire to wash our dishes in the neighbor's pool.
kotecki

Stinky Speaks

This burgeoning super-sizing sensation is way beyond being out-of-control. We saw an elderly lady in aisle five struggling to hoist a gigantic bag of dog food that looked more like a raft that could comfortably accommodate a dozen refugees than a bag of Kibbles 'n Bits. I was waiting for her to snap something.

And why do I have a feeling that the lucky dog is one of those scrawny pint-sized canines with a cute name like Powder Puff or Princess?

Mom! This one looks good...
kotecki
www.KimandJason.com © 2004 by Jason W. Kotecki
RUMBLE
RUMBLE
ORANGES
...Don't you think?
Definitely. The rest are all bruised...

Stinky Speaks

Clean-up on aisle seven...

I know it's stupid, but I love reading supermarket tabloids.
When Liz Taylor marries a dead alien, I like to be informed.
And it's much easier to plan your week when you know the end of the world is this Wednesday.
kotecki
www.KimandJason.com © 2004 by Jason W. Kotecki
MOM! That guy has THREE arms!
Ah, journalism at its finest.
TRABLO
INQUIRY

Stinky Speaks

Dick Clark is really 145 years old? Believe it! Thirty-five Martians took the form of Tony Danza and built a Wal-Mart is Poughkeepsie? Who knew? A new can't miss diet featuring a steady stream of Twinkies and Diet Coke? Sign me up!

Childhood Is...
Riding In A Shopping Cart.
www.KimandJason.com © 2004 by Jason W. Kotecki
Aw c'mon **DAD** does wheelies!
kotecki

Stinky Speaks

This conversation could get really interesting if Kim happens to mention the time "Daredevil Dad" accidentally took out an entire end cap of Little Debbie snack cakes and an unsuspecting teenage stock boy...

I don't really mind these trips to the supermarket.
Sure, I'm not big on crowds, and I find their selection of exotic fruits deplorable...
...but at least I can always count on some snippet of entertainment.
kotecki
www.KimandJason.com © 2004 by Jason W. Kotecki
MOM!-- It looks like that guy swallowed an ELEPHANT!
POTATO PUFFS
Reality TV, eat your heart out.

THE EAVESDROPPER

Is there any modern household item that incites such division and causes such sibling upheaval as the telephone? If this episode is any indication, probably not.

...Oh, I know...tell me about it...
Of course she likes him. It's like, so obvious.
BEEP BIP BEEP BEEP BIP BEEP BIP
Hold on a sec.
I'M ON THE PHONE!
Your phone is rude.
www.KimandJason.com © 2004 by Jason W. Kotecki
I can't call home 'cause your sister's on the phone.
I guess I'll have to wait.
Just tell her to get off.
No WAY! Last time she gave me a wedgie!
And this pair of underpants is already a little tight.
www.KimandJason.com © 2004 by Jason W. Kotecki
I'll do all the talking.
KATIE! Jason needs to use the phone to call his Mom!
KNOCK KNOCK
And I need to hear what Johnny Romano said about Jessica Stevens!
BEAT IT.
Looks like she'll be doing all the talking.
I'd give anything for a stun gun right now.
www.KimandJason.com © 2004 by Jason W. Kotecki
kotecki

"I'd give anything for a stun gun right now."

I think Katie is STILL on the phone!
Who is she talking to?
We're about to find out...
I don't think you should be doing that!
Shhh... I do it all the time.
www.KimandJason.com © 2004 by Jason W. Kotecki
That's how I found out "going sweaty" means only dating one person.
Kotecki

KATIE! YOU'VE BEEN ON THE PHONE FOR TWO HOURS! GET OFF NOW!
www.KimandJason.com © 2004 by Jason W. Kotecki
Is she off?
I can't tell... It's quiet.
Maybe you made her cry...
Kotecki

"Going sweaty means only dating one person."

Childhood is...
Eavesdropping On Your Older Sister.
www.KimandJason.com © 2004 by Jason W. Kotecki
She's talking about kissing a BOY?
...from France, I think...
Kotecki

Katie is STILL on the phone!
SLAM
What's so important for her to talk about?
Who knows!
But, if it's SO IMPORTANT...
CLICK
REC PLAY
...I think EVERYBODY should be able to hear it!
kotecki
www.KimandJason.com © 2004 by Jason W. Kotecki

THE CHALKBOARD
Share your sibling war stories...

"My brother used to tease me, and I wouldn't do much about it. Then one day he went past the point and I hit him on the head with a pan. I was little at the time."
Michelle, age 24
Minnesota

"When doing dishes, my older sister Carrie was ALWAYS the washer and I was ALWAYS the dryer and put-awayer. I would beg her to just give me a chance at the washer gig. However, she never found it in her heart to hand me the dishrag and soap. One day, we were home by ourselves and my mom instructed us to clean up the kitchen while she was gone. I saw this as the golden opportunity to get back at my sister. On the stove was a large pot that had leftover mashed potatoes in it. I grabbed that pot and a spoon and fired away at my unsuspecting sister. She was definitely in shock when the day-old taters hit her square in the face! My sister then grabbed a spoon of her own and whipped a couple spoonfuls at me. Before long, potatoes filled our hair, our clothes, the kitchen cabinets, counters, and floor. I remember we were flicking mashed potatoes to the beat of Phil Collins. My mom came home to find an immaculately clean kitchen and she was none the wiser about our food battle!"
Connie Kotecki, age 25
Harvard, IL

"I am the oldest of three children. My younger brother, Michael, was big on teasing and instigating fights, especially with Missy who was younger. And if my brother would fall or trip or hurt himself as a result of the fights, my mom did not have much sympathy for her son, the bully. She would always say: "See Michael, God punished you for fighting." There was one time in particular that Michael and Missy were chasing each other around the house. Soon, my mom heard Missy crying and called Michael into the kitchen and asked him why she was crying. "Did you hit your sister?" she asked. And matter of factly, he replied, "No mom, she was chasing me, so God punched her."
Marci Jezierski, age 22
DeKalb, IL

THE UNCLEAN ROOM

In real life, Kim is pretty organized. But she can be a bit of a "piler." It doesn't take much time for these piles to take over and resemble the aftermath of a natural disaster. In the strip, a messy room is a Kim staple, and her method for dealing with them consists of creating new piles and covering up old ones.

I don't know why I have to clean my room.
Mysteries of life are not easily solved.
It's not like it's even DIRTY...
kotecki
www.KimandJason.com © 2004 by Jason W. Kotecki
...it just happens to have a lot of things in it!
Your room looks like a Wal-Mart right after a shopping spree by a suburban family of F-5 tornados.

Stinky Speaks

Actually, Wal-Mart doesn't need help from any natural disasters to look like your upstairs closet that hasn't been organized since thin ties were fashionable.

The prices may be unbeatable, but they could use a little help in the design department. When I'm forced to go into a Wal-Mart (you don't think I'd go there willingly, do you?), I feel like I'm being shouted at, thanks to the over-abundance of gaudy, mismatched signs.

What's next? Televisions screaming commercials at shoppers who are just trying to find their way to the laundry soap?...oh, wait, they thought of that one already, haven't they...

Hello? I need Super J's help...
REALLY? OK! You've come to the right place, citizen!
kotecki
Super J is capable of anything, afraid of nothing, and is very handsome.
www.KimandJason.com © 2004 by Jason W. Kotecki
Look, my room is messy, and I need--
Sorry. Wrong number.
click.

Cleaning this room is going to take me forever!
Forever is a stretch, but I'd agree with decades.
www.KimandJason.com
What's the point of cleaning it? Am I supposed to learn something from this?
I'm just going to mess it up again anyway!
© 2004 by Jason W. Kotecki
kotecki
Learning - now I can see how THAT could take forever.

Stinky Speaks

I'd like to take this opportunity to ask God to bless the unrelenting teachers who engage in a daily battle to reach the minds of children who seem to have skulls made of petrified cherry wood.

Boompa, why does my room have to be clean?
People with clean rooms have higher chances of eating ice cream.
REALLY? Is that true?
Oh yes. It's widely known.
© 2004 by Jason W. Kotecki
WOW! C'mon Stinky - let's get busy!
Thanks, Boompa! You're so smart!
www.KimandJason.com
Some would say experienced.
kotecki

Stinky Speaks

Question of the day: Under the full realization that Ben & Jerry's New York Super Fudge Chunk is quite rich, at what age does the currency of sugary dairy desserts finally give way to the currency of gold and stock options? Because it seems to carry an abnormally high value to five-year-olds.

Mom, do you have any clean sheets?
Clean sheets? Wow. You're really doing a good job on your room!
www.KimandJason.com © 2004 by Jason W. Kotecki
Who knew it could be so easy to clean my room AND impress Mom!
It really opens up the space.
kotecki

Stinky Speaks

What's also quite nice with this method of organization is that the space under the bed is conveniently left open to store discarded candy wrappers, random puzzle pieces, and half-eaten apples.

Childhood Is...
Cleaning Your Room.
The hardest part is figuring out where to start.
YIKES. This is quite a mess.
I think I'll start by watching cartoons.
kotecki

Stinky Speaks

Honestly, I think the cartoon-watching idea is the best bet in this situation. At this point, I think Kim can do nothing but make the problem much, much worse. I think we'd all be better served by closing the door, leaving the immediate vicinity, and praying for a miraculous visit from the Tooth Fairy's mysterious and unheralded half-sibling, the Room Cleaning Fairy.

How'd it go cleaning your room?
Fine. I'm all finished, at least.
kotecki
Really? That didn't take very long.
I've got a system down.
Wait. Did you just stuff everything under your bed?
WHAT?! No.. that's crazy!
www.KimandJason.com © 2004 by Jason W. Kotecki
My bed is not THAT big!
But it took a long time just to get my closet doors to stay shut.

THE PUDDLE JUMPERS

Here is an undeniable truth: The surest sign that you are officially an adult is when you start habitually walking *around* puddles rather than blasting *through* them.

PLOP
kotecki
www.KimandJason.com © 2004 by Jason W. Kotecki
Uh-oh. Looks like rain. We better go in.
Don't be so wimpy. A little rain never hurt nobody.
Said Noah's critics.

Stinky Speaks

Seriously though, let's get inside before the flood comes. If you think wet dogs smell bad after they've been outdoors, can you imagine a skunk?

But more importantly, I don't want to have to do my hair all over again.

Hey, I can see my reflection in this puddle!
Neat!
www.KimandJason.com © 2004 by Jason W. Kotecki
I think looking at water is peaceful.
How 'bout you?
Too peaceful!
kotecki

Have you ever skipped rocks in the water?
No, how do you do it?
Like this...
www.KimandJason.com © 2004 by Jason W. Kotecki
kotecki
Nice one!
So does hitting moving cars give you extra points or something?
SKIP

Ready?
www.KimandJason.com © 2004 by Jason W. Kotecki
Now THAT was fun!
Puddles are one of the best toys God ever made!
Boy, we got pretty WET!
www.KimandJason.com © 2004 by Jason W. Kotecki
We're gonna get in trouble!
Maybe YOU will...
...But I didn't go outside without MY raincoat.
KOTECKI

> Puddles are one of the best toys God ever made!

Childhood IS...
Testing The Buoyancy Of Objects.
www.KimandJason.com © 2004 by Jason W. Kotecki
Well?
Well? Am I floating?
KOTECKI

Hey–look! A rainbow!
I don't know how it can call itself a rainbow.
It's not even TIED.
Kotecki
www.KimandJason.com © 2004 by Jason W. Kotecki

"Don't you moms ever take the day off?"

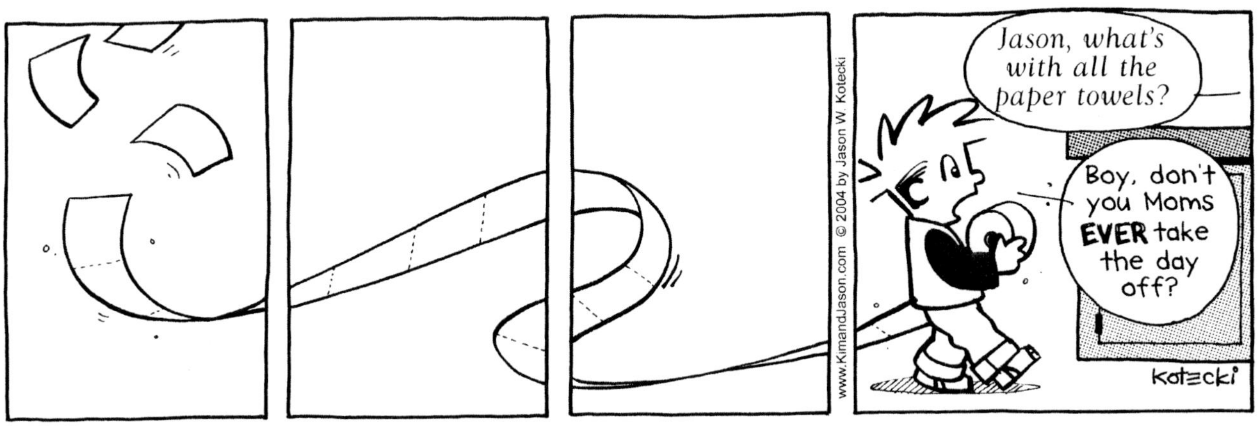
www.KimandJason.com © 2004 by Jason W. Kotecki
Jason, what's with all the paper towels?
Boy, don't you Moms EVER take the day off?
Kotecki

Can you pass the blue egg die?
Here you go...
What's so funny?
Nothing.
Ha Ha APRIL FOOLS! That's not blew-- it's PURPLE!
I thought something seemed strange.
You've been PUNKED!
How many misteaks YOU find?
© 2004 by Jason W. Kotecki
www.KimandJason.com
Kotecki

OFFICIAL ANSWERS FOR THE 4TH ANNUAL APRIL FOOLS DAY CONTEST

Panel #1
The "?" is backwards
"Dye" is misspelled

Panel #2
Jason has "Elvis" hair
There is an arrow through Kim's word balloon
Kim is wearing a halo
Kim is also wearing a baseball mitt
Jason has a "9" on his shirt
Jason's egg is now a baseball

Panel #3
"Blue" is misspelled
Kim is wearing a swimsuit
There is a bird in the cup
The cup design is different
The spilled egg dye is now gone

Panel #4
Jason is wearing a star headband
The stripes on Jason's shirt are missing
Kim has brown hair
"Mistake" is misspelled
The word "can" is missing from the sentence
"How many mistakes can you find?"

What's HE here for?
To help us color Easter eggs!
Oh, thank heavens! What would we EVER do without him?
kotecki
Don't mind her--
She's just being sartastic.
Sartastic?
That's like a mean version of fantastic.
© 2004 by Jason W. Kotecki
www.KimandJason.com

sartastic: a poem by kim

katie is sartastik
NOT fantastik
I know it is drastik
but i wish she was plastik

www.KimandJason.com © 2004 by Jason W. Kotecki
Isn't this FUN, Stinky?
What could be more fun than misaligned internal organs?
LOOK! The merry-go-round is free!
kotecki

Stinky Speaks

Now I finally know what it feels like to have one's innards pureed in a blender like a banana daiquiri.

Lucky me.

If you write on your egg with white crayon first, it'll show up after you put it in the dye.
Really?
What are you writing on yours?
www.KimandJason.com © 2004 by Jason W. Kotecki
How should I know? I can't see it!
kotecki

Childhood Is...
Coloring Easter Eggs.
www.KimandJason.com © 2004 by Jason W. Kotecki
We don't have any yellow ones yet!
Don't worry! We still have four naked ones over here.
kotecki

kotecki
KIM! What have you done -- I'm all green!
This will NEVER come out...
...I'll be green my ENTIRE life...
...no boy will come near me...
!
www.KimandJason.com © 2004 by Jason W. Kotecki
...and I'll be the laughing stock of the whole school!
KIM!
Did you hear me? I SAID pass the green already!

THE EASTER BUNNY LETTERS

I gotta say, I really had a good time writing this episode. I love getting deep into Kim's mind, and exploring her thought processing. i also appreciated the opportunity to get down on paper some the questions about the Easter Bunny that I myself have had for so long.

What are you doing?
Writing a letter to the Easter Bunny.
I didn't know you could do that.
Why not? I'm sure he can read!
But where will you send it?
The North Pole.
I'm sure Santa will get it to him.
kotecki
www.KimandJason.com © 2004 by Jason W. Kotecki

"I'm sure all those guys hang out together during the off-season." -- Kim

Dear Easter Bunny...
This is my first letter to you so I have lots of questions.
But first things first.
Are you allowed to put puppies in Easter baskets?
kotecki
www.KimandJason.com © 2004 by Jason W. Kotecki

"Maybe there should be two baskets, because I don't want my puppy eating all my jelly beans." -- Kim

Dear Easter Bunny, here's one for you.
How do you get to all the kids houses?
Santa has the slay and rainder. What do you have?
Or do you just rent all that stuff from him?
kotecki
www.KimandJason.com © 2004 by Jason W. Kotecki

"Maybe the Easter Bunny could get himself a hot air balloon. It's even got a basket right on it. He could put some green grass in it for cushioning." -- Kim

Dear Easter Bunny. Do you have a list like Santa?
You know, with the good and bad boys and girls.
If yer mad about that little insident with Katie, you'll have to talk to God about that one.
He's the one who decided to make big sisters.
kotecki
www.KimandJason.com © 2004 by Jason W. Kotecki

"Seriously, big sisters weren't one of God's better ideas." -- Kim

Dear Easter Bunny
Can you give me some hints about where you'll be hiding eggs this year?
Katie always finds them first.
Just leev a little map under my pillow (ask the Tooth Fairy for help if you need to.)
kotecki
www.KimandJason.com © 2004 by Jason W. Kotecki

"Maybe he could put a fake map under Katie's pillow. She deserves it." -- Kim

Childhood Is...
Staying Up Late To Catch The Easter Bunny.
www.KimandJason.com © 2004 by Jason W. Kotecki
ZZZZ
kotecki

Dear Easter Bunny, how did you get yer job?
Was there any other animals up for it or just you?
Did you ntervyou for the Christmas job?
Do you Know Santa? Whats He really like?
What will happin when you retire?
Maybe you could put in a good word for my frend Stinky.
I think he'd be a good one to have in charge of some holiday.
Ask him what Arbor Day pays.
Kotecki
www.KimandJason.com © 2004 by Jason W. Kotecki

THE ERRAND RUNNER

This episode gives Kim another opportunity to be one-on-one with Boompa. Not only does it allow Kim to ask lots of questions, it gives me an opportunity to draw Boompa's truck. I have a photo I found of an old 1952 Chevy truck that I've loosely based my rendition of Boompa's transportation. I think some of those old-time cars are so cool, and I love drawing it hurling through midair. I don't know if it's possible for anything that old to still be running – not to mention how many miles it would have – but I just can't picture Boompa in a Hummer. I guess I always figured that Boompa would be mechanically inclined enough to keep a classic like that in tip-top shape.

All buckled up, Kim?
Yep!
Are we there yet?
Kim, we haven't even left the driveway.
Sorry-habit.
kot≡cki www.KimandJason.com © 2004 by Jason W. Kotecki

Hey Boompa!
kot≡cki
It's kind of like you're the pilot and I'm the co-pilot!
Yep – kind of.
www.KimandJason.com © 2004 by Jason W. Kotecki
Wanna switch?

Boompa! You're driving like an old man --step on it!
kot≡cki
Does it make any difference that I AM an old man?
Boompa... you're not that old to me.
www.KimandJason.com © 2004 by Jason W. Kotecki
Now pick up the pace– we're about to get passed by a kid on a skateboard!

Boompa, did people always drive around in cars?
Actually, no. We used horses before that.
© 2004 by Jason W. Kotecki • www.KimandJason.com
But how did they fit the horse in the car?
kotecki

Boompa, how does a person know what they'll look like when they get old?
Well, you don't really.
So it's like a surprise, then?
You could say that.
www.KimandJason.com © 2004 by Jason W. Kotecki
kotecki
How 'bout those wrinkles? Did they surprise you all at once?

Childhood Is...
Going On Errands With Grandpa.
www.KimandJason.com © 2004 by Jason W. Kotecki
I like riding with you in your truck, Boompa.
Well, that was awfully nice of you to say.
It's the only time I get to ride in the front seat.
kotecki

“How did they fit the horse in the car?”

It's not fair that they don't let kids my age drive.
Well, I --
It's an invasion of privacy!
No, not exa--
What about my RIGHTS?
Rights?
I mean, what's the point of the Conspitution?
I don't think there's any-thing in there about --
Why did Abeham Lincoln write it if no one pays attention to it?
But he--
What do YOU think, Boompa?
I think I'll plead the fifth.
Oh, sure! Fifth graders can drive, not ME?
Kotecki
www.KimandJason.com © 2004 by Jason W. Kotecki

THE EXPLORERS

When doing a strip about children, it's not necessary to figure out ways to get them into exotic locals for an exciting adventure. Excitement, intrigue, and danger are usually not too far away. Kids only need to look as far as the backyard.

Ready to go explore?
Where should we start?
Our choices are limited.
Why can't we live anywhere cool?
I wish they'd tear down the mall and put up a jungle.
kotecki
www.KimandJason.com © 2004 by Jason W. Kotecki

Kim: "Or at least put up one of those restaurants with the jungle right inside."

HEY! Looky here!
Amazing! What could it be?
A primitive writing tool?
A bone from an extinct animal?
Who knows? But doesn't it look like rubber when I do this?
kotecki
www.KimandJason.com © 2004 by Jason W. Kotecki

Jason: "What if that was a fragile artifact, like a dinosaur bone?"
Kim: "I don't know...are dinosaur bones made of rubber?"

Hmm... footprints!
KIM! Our first real break-through!
I wonder where they lead!
Huh?
kotecki
www.KimandJason.com © 2004 by Jason W. Kotecki

Jason: "I can't believe I got my hopes up for a set of footprints made by you."
Kim: "Hey, in a million years, those footprints might be worth something, buster."

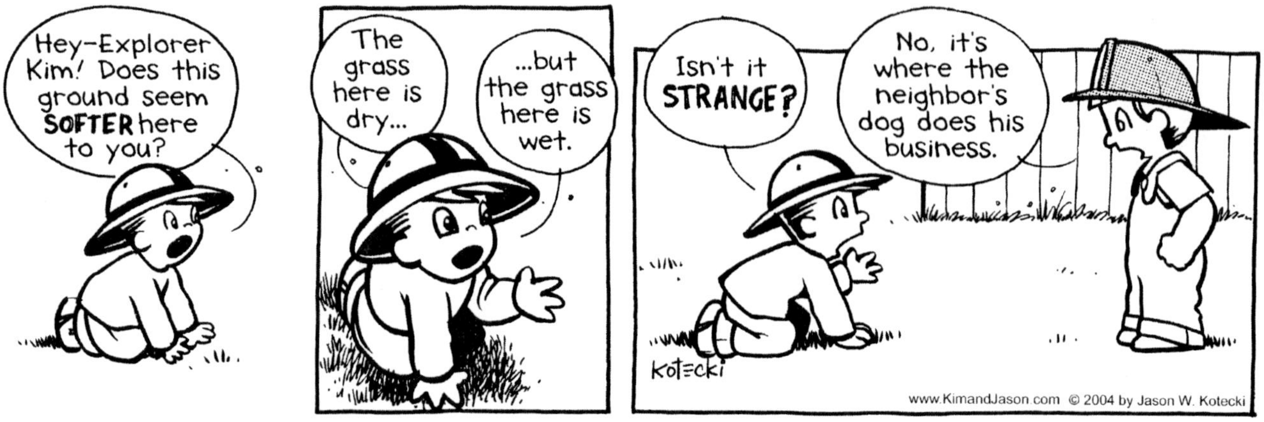
Hey–Explorer Kim! Does this ground seem SOFTER here to you?
The grass here is dry...
...but the grass here is wet.
Isn't it STRANGE?
No, it's where the neighbor's dog does his business.
KOTECKI
www.KimandJason.com © 2004 by Jason W. Kotecki

Kim: "...and when I say 'business,' I don't mean the kind with ties and computers and those little suitcases."

LOOK!- I found a popsicle® stick!
© 2004 by Jason W. Kotecki
Do you know what this MEANS?
www.KimandJason.com
It proves that there were popsicles® in ancient times.
No, smarty.
It only proves that there were popsicle® STICKS in ancient times.
KOTECKI

Jason: "What would people in ancient time do with popsicle sticks besides make Popsicles®?"
Kim: "I don't know, maybe they used them to make little houses for a school project."

Childhood Is...
Exploring The Backyard.
www.KimandJason.com © 2004 by Jason W. Kotecki
We need to explore every inch of this area for clues.
8
Are ANTS clues?
KOTECKI

"Are ants clues?"

We're going out exploring, Mom!
If we're not back in a few hours, call the lifeguard.
Lifeguard?
Coast guard?
No.
National guard?
No.
Point guard?
No.
Sneeze guard?
No...
JUST CALL THE POLICE!
www.KimandJason.com © 2004 by Jason W. Kotecki
kotecki

Who are we kidding? There's nothing exciting out here.
www.KimandJason.com © 2004 by Jason W. Kotecki
We need to explore some new territory.
But your Mom said to stay in the backyard.
No, she said to stay where she can see us.
kotecki

Jason: "We're gonna get in trouble for sure..."
Kim: "How can we? We're doing exactly what she said. Although I guess she might get mad about the wallpaper that came off the wall with my picture...but she'll never notice once I put it back."

C,mon- let's go!
Where are we going?
To explore some far away land.
Oooo! Like Jupiter?
Does this LOOK like a spaceship?
www.KimandJason.com © 2004 by Jason W. Kotecki
kotecki

Kim: "My spaceship is in the shop."

Go to: dess
I've adjusted the settings. The destination is set!
Kim! Desert only has one "s"– you just spelled "dessert!"
We don't want to end up in a chocolate cake!
We don't?
www.KimandJason.com © 2004 by Jason W. Kotecki
kotecki

Kim: "How about a big bowl of Cool Whip® – would you say yes to that?"

I gotta work on my landings.
www.KimandJason.com © 2004 by Jason W. Kotecki
kotecki

Kim: "Those landings are tricky. I think my landing gear is broken."
Jason: "I think one of my livers is broken..."

“I gotta work on my landings.”

I've collected some great samples of sand!
Good. We can look at it under our nuclear powered microscope back at the lab.
But we don't have one of those.
And we have my Aunt Emily to thank for that.
I've **NEVER** asked for socks for my birthday.
www.KimandJason.com © 2004 by Jason W. Kotecki
kotecki

Jason: “If only I had a nuclear powered microscope for every pair of socks I've gotten for my birthday, I'd...”
Kim: “Be the world's biggest nerd?”

If I didn't know better, I'd swear we were on another planet.
Like Canada?
A place like this really makes you think...
How does life survive out here?
Was this **ALWAYS** a desert?
Why did God **MAKE** deserts?
What do **YOU** think, Kim?
Hold on. I keep getting sand in my shoe.
kotecki
www.KimandJason.com © 2004 by Jason W. Kotecki

Childhood is...
Exploring Far-Off Lands.
kotecki
www.KimandJason.com © 2004 by Jason W. Kotecki
Deserts are a real shame.
Just a little water and you could make the world's biggest sandcastle!

When we decided to fly to the desert, I thought there would be a lot more to explore.
So far, all we've collected is sand and rocks.
I haven't seen anything here that I can't see in my own backyard.
kotecki www.KimandJason.com © 2004 by Jason W. Kotecki

Jason: "How long before we find something bigger than a stupid pebble? An eternity?"
Kim: "It better not take that long; I have to go in before it gets dark."

Um, Jason?
What?
www.KimandJason.com © 2004 by Jason W. Kotecki
Look up!
Is it just me, or is that a dinosaur?
No, it's not just you...
It's you, me, AND a dinosaur!
kotecki

Jason: "How did he get here?"
Kim: "Well I'm not gonna ask him. Do you speak dinosaur?"

I can't figure out why this dinosaur is in the desert.
He's a plant eater, but there are no plants around!
Maybe your books are wrong.
He seems to like candy bars just fine.
kotecki
www.KimandJason.com © 2004 by Jason W. Kotecki
He?
I named him Gary.

Jason: "How do you even know he's a boy?"
Kim: "He sure smells like one to me."

Even if your Mom is okay with bringing a dinosaur home...
www.KimandJason.com © 2004 by Jason W. Kotecki
I don't think he'll fit in the plane.
kotecki
What did your Mom FEED you, Gary?
I never knew that eating my vegetables could make me THAT big...

Jason: "This is not going to make me start eating asparagus."
Kim: "Not wheelbarrows full of it, at least."

We're home!
kotecki
www.KimandJason.com © 2004 by Jason W. Kotecki
It's too bad we had to leave Gary the dinosaur behind.
He's prob'ly better off in his own habitat.

Jason: "We wouldn't have anyplace to keep him, anyway."
Kim: "If I cleaned up my bedroom, he could probably sleep on the floor in there. So long, Gary."

Childhood Is...
Imagining The Ultimate pet.
www.KimandJason.com © 2004 by Jason W. Kotecki
Kotecki

If HE couldn't make it, what chance do WE have?
Maybe if he had a few more salads he would've lived longer.
Kotecki
www.KimandJason.com © 2004 by Jason W. Kotecki

When you're around children as much as I am, you learn many things...
www.KimandJason.com © 2004 by Jason W. Kotecki
Things I'm not sure I'd learn anywhere else...
WoW! Thirty seconds!
A new record!
...Like how long the average pancake will stick to the ceiling.
kotecki

Stinky Speaks

It'll stay up there even longer if you coat it with some stale maple syrup before tossing it skyward.

I love maple syrup.
kotecki
The real, straight-from-the-tree, non-diluted, concentrated kind.
C'mon, it's MY turn!
Not THAT concentrated.
www.KimandJason.com © 2004 by Jason W. Kotecki

Stinky Speaks

This reminds me of the time they drank thirty-five packets of Kool-Aid® powder. And washed it down with Jolt® Cola. I then witnessed firsthand what it would look like if pinballs were alive and the size of five-year-olds.

Like anyone else, I enjoy listening to music to unwind.
www.KimandJason.com © 2004 by Jason W. Kotecki
I'm preferential to the smooth sounds of Sinatra, but I'm pretty open-minded.
HIS NAME IS MY NAME TOOO
kotecki
...Except when it comes to songs involving John Jacob Jingleheimer Schmidt.

Stinky Speaks

I am also of the belief that music is meant to be sung, not shouted at the top of one's lungs, as if in competition with the volume of a 747 on take off.

Technology is developing at an increasingly rapid pace.
www.KimandJason.com © 2004 by Jason W. Kotecki
Boompa, all you have to do is push this button, then this one, wait for the light to blink twice, and push "enter".
Easy!
kotecki
Ever get the feeling that you're not developing at quite the same pace?

Stinky Speaks

Remember when VCRs were $900? Or when cordless phones were the size of a Shaquille O'Neal shoe? When 8-tracks were all the rage?

Fasten your seatbelts, folks. We'll be commuting with the Jetsons before you know it.

Wars have been waged since the dawn of time.
kotecki
www.KimandJason.com © 2004 by Jason W. Kotecki
You can argue whether they were justified or necessary.
It's mine! I found it!
It's my house, and MY cereal!
But I doubt few were as fierce as a dispute over who gets the cereal box prize.

Stinky Speaks

And if that prize should happen to glow in the dark, stockpile rations and run for cover.

Childhood is...
Mysterious Lunchtime Foods.
www.KimandJason.com © 2004 by Jason W. Kotecki
More, please!
Me too!
Question.
Since when do chickens have fingers?
8
kotecki

It is my estimation that people who don't have kids seriously underestimate the cost of HAVING kids.
kotecki
Most people factor in food...
CREAM PIZZA
...and clothes...
...and even the accessories.
But what about the incidentals?
RRRRRKRRKRRRRRR
MOM-- A spoon fell down the drain and I accidentally turned on the garbage disposal!
Take plumbing, for instance.

THE T-BALL PLAYERS

Yes, in real life, I did play t-ball. For about two minutes.

My mom took me to play t-ball, and being the shy youngster that I was, I became completely overwhelmed by the whole situation. There were lots of strange kids I didn't know, all of whom seemed to be way more confident than me. I was, to put it mildly, a little intimidated. I left the dugout and told my Mom that I wanted to go home. I didn't play organized baseball again until I was ten years old.

This was a very difficult episode to write. Even though I allowed myself to not be too shackled to the real life occurrences of this event, I still had to confront the fears I felt on my first day of t-ball. I'm still not exactly sure what my problem was. And I'm certain I didn't reach any psychological breakthroughs through the process...but at least I made it through the episode without any significant bills from a therapist.

I love art.

I had been wanting to do a t-ball episode for quite some time. Upon having the chance, I soon realized that if I stuck too close to real life, this would be one of the shortest episodes ever. And so I let go and let the "character" Jason write the rest of this episode for me...

Mom, did you sign me up for t-ball yet?
Yep. Just this morning.
Good. What kind of signing bonus did you get us?
I need a new agent.
kotecki
www.KimandJason.com © 2004 by Jason W. Kotecki

"Moms make a good pot roast, but they make horrible agents. I bet she didn't even get me a no-trade clause." -- Jason

Do you want my autograph?
Why?
Now that I'm a big sports star, it'll really be worth a lot.
A big sports star?
Did I say big? I meant HUGE.
Just because your Mom signed you up for T-Ball?
You can watch for yourself.
The games will prob'ly be on ESPN.
kotecki
www.KimandJason.com © 2004 by Jason W. Kotecki

"I'm sure my highlights will end up on Sportscenter." -- Jason

So what's t-ball like?
It's like baseball.
www.KimandJason.com © 2004 by Jason W. Kotecki
kotecki
How about the tea parties - when do they start?
There's NO tea parties!
That's a shame. t-ball almost sounded fun.

"I thought maybe they set the tables and chairs up on that nice little hill in the middle of the field." -- Kim

I think I might have my Mom sign me up for t-ball too!
YOU? I thought you HATED baseball!
Well, I'm not too good at dribbling, but I like the outfits.
Uniforms. They're called UNIFORMS.
www.KimandJason.com © 2004 by Jason W. Kotecki
Whatever.
I hope I get on a red team.
kotecki

"Even if it's not a red team, I just hope it's not a pea green team. That would make me not like baseball very much at all." -- Kim

Guess who's on your t-ball team?
SAMMY SOSA?
kotecki
No, silly-- ME!
Oh.
www.KimandJason.com © 2004 by Jason W. Kotecki
I thought you'd be happier.
If they allowed trades in t-ball, I would be.

"Or maybe we could send her down to the minors, but I'm pretty sure t-ball doesn't have those either." -- Jason

Childhood Is...
Playing Catch With Yourself.
www.KimandJason.com © 2004 by Jason W. Kotecki
Stupid gutters.
Kotecki

Here you go!
What's this?
You hold in your hands a RARE and VALUABLE collectible.
A crayon drawing?
Kotecki
No!-- It's my ROOKIE CARD!
Oh.
And its value will skyrocket once I am abducted into the Hall of Fame!
Just be sure to keep it away from your Mom.
© 2004 by Jason W. Kotecki
They have a habit of throwing things like this away.
www.KimandJason.com

If you're gonna be on my t-ball team, I can't have you stinking up the joint.
Why would you think that?
If the coach told you to play right field, would you even know where that is?
Yes!
www.KimandJason.com © 2004 by Jason W. Kotecki
As soon as he tells me where the wrong one is.
Kotecki

So how much kicking is involved in t-ball?
None. There's no kicking in baseball.
Oh, right. Now, are girls allowed to play quarter-back?
That's FOOTBALL! Do you even know ANYTHING about baseball?
What!
Maybe you should wait to ask me that AFTER you see all the slam dunks I get.
www.KimandJason.com © 2004 by Jason W. Kotecki
kotecki

"By the way...how many slam dunks is good?" -- Kim

Let's see what you got!
www.KimandJason.com © 2004 by Jason W. Kotecki
The problem is that you throw like a girl.
Well, what do I look like, a BIG STINKY BOY?
kotecki

T-ball is starting soon. We've got a lot of work to do so you don't embarass yourself...
Why? Are the uniforms bad? They're not pea green, are they?
...or me.
www.KimandJason.com © 2004 by Jason W. Kotecki
Pea green uniforms will embarass us all!
kotecki

Childhood Is...
Backyard Baseball.
www.KimandJason.com © 2004 by Jason W. Kotecki
Okay, so over the neighbor's fence is a home run.
Right. And into the neighbor's window is a run home.
kotecki

When it comes down to it, coaches are teachers.
What separates the good ones from the bad ones?
www.KimandJason.com © 2004 by Jason W. Kotecki
No! You won't be tackled when you hit it! NOW SWING!
kotecki
That would be the calm, cool poise exhibited when patience is stretched thinner than a flu-ridden Calista Flockhart.

Stinky Speaks

Not thin enough for you? How about thinner than the toilet paper you'll find in the roadside bathroom of a 7-11 in the middle of winter.

kotecki
www.KimandJason.com
© 2004 by Jason W. Kotecki
Shouldn't you be practicing?
I am! I'm practicing what it will be like when I hit a home run to win the game!

"Hey, do they allow limousines out on the field during the game?" -- Kim

Hey, how many players are on a baseball team?
www.KimandJason.com © 2004 by Jason W. Kotecki
There are nine players on a team and you play for nine innings.
Each team gets three outs per inning.
kotecki
Woah, woah, woah -- I didn't ask for a story problem!

"Jeez -- what kind of sport requires a calculator?" -- Kim

Hey Katie! Wanna play?
Heck no. I wanted to see what it looked like when two dufuses play baseball.
Didja hear that, Jason?
A FAN!
Ok, throw me a high one!
THUD
Oops... I lost it in the clouds.
Painful... Great, that's two minutes I'll NEVER get back.
Hey! Where are you going?
To go find your baseball card on eBay so I can have you autograph it.
Wait! Maybe Jason can draw one for you!
kotecki
www.KimandJason.com © 2004 by Jason W. Kotecki

Nice shot, Jason!
kotecki
www.KimandJason.com © 2004 by Jason W. Kotecki
You're supposed to catch it!
SORRY! I was thinking we were playing mini-golf.
You missed your calling as a croquet wicket.

"We need one of those windmill thingys. Maybe we could put it by second base." -- Kim

Check it out! My Mom picked up my t-ball outfit today!
kotecki
www.KimandJason.com © 2004 by Jason W. Kotecki
Can you believe it -- it's RED!
Where's the rest of it?
What?
The pants, the hat, the stirrups...
This is it. I'm wearing leotards with mine.
No metal spikes either, I take it.

Babe Ruth DID NOT wear Levi's.
www.KimandJason.com © 2004 by Jason W. Kotecki
I can't believe I have to wear jeans as part of my baseball uniform!
Tell me about it. My Mom said no to the leotard.
kotecki
Or a LEOTARD, for that matter.

Childhood IS... Your First Uniform.
8
www.KimandJason.com © 2004 by Jason W. Kotecki
My Mom let me get some baseball pants and a baseball glove!
Now I look like a REAL baseball player.
Let the endorsement deals roll in!
The black marker is a nice touch.
kotecki

"I didn't want it to rub off while I was playing, so I used the permanent kind." -- Jason

Ready for some pop-ups?
Sure!
Better go deeper. I don't want to hit it over your head!
kotecki
www.KimandJason.com © 2004 by Jason W. Kotecki
THUD
THUD
Should I move in some?
At least then I could enjoy the breeze!

HURRY UP, MOM! We've got to get over to the t-ball field!
I want to get there early.
I like to sign autographs during batting practice.
kotecki
www.KimandJason.com © 2004 by Jason W. Kotecki

"Anything to make my fans happy." -- Jason

WOW! I didn't know how many new friends I'd make!
Woah. I didn't know how many strangers would be here.
kotecki
www.KimandJason.com © 2004 by Jason W. Kotecki

I always get nervous in new situations.
I think I want my Mom to drive me home.
But I guess everybody here is prob'ly a little nervous.
LOOK EVERYBODY! My head is a baseball!
kotecki
www.KimandJason.com © 2004 by Jason W. Kotecki

I'm a nervous wreck.
What am I so afraid of?
Everybody here seems nice. I'll prob'ly just blend right in.
Hey Jason! Did you remember to wear your lucky Spiderman underpants?
kotecki
www.KimandJason.com © 2004 by Jason W. Kotecki

Boy, you look PALE.
I'm just a little nervous, that's all.
ATTENTION EVERYBODY!
My friend Jason is a little nervous, so everybody be real nice to him. He's not usually this white.
Or red.
kotecki
www.KimandJason.com
© 2004 by Jason W. Kotecki

Childhood Is...
Chants From The Dugout.
www.KimandJason.com © 2004 by Jason W. Kotecki
WE WANT A PITCHER, NOT A BELLY ITCHER!
This is t-ball. There is no pitcher.
kotecki
WE WANT A TEE, NOT A BELLY ITCHER!

www.KimandJason.com
© 2004 by Jason W. Kotecki
BONK
Oops! I need a do-over!
kotecki

Timmy, this is my best friend Jason. He's a little nervous.
www.KimandJason.com © 2004 by Jason W. Kotecki
I'm nervous, too.
Really?
Uh-huh.
See? Nothing to be ashamed of!
Now, which of you two nervous nellies has seen my glove?
kotecki

"C'mon worry warts, get off your duffs and help me find my glove already." -- Kim

So you're nervous like **ME**, Timmy?
Yep. There's a lot of people here that I don't know.
My Mom said I'd make friends... but I'm too shy.
kotecki
www.KimandJason.com © 2004 by Jason W. Kotecki
ME Too! And that's what **MY** Mom said!
Hmpf. I guess Moms don't know every-thing.
You said it.

"It makes me wonder if she knows what she's talking about when she says vegetables are good for you." -- Jason

I'm up to bat next. Any last minute tips?
Keep your eye on the ball.
Swing hard!
kotecki
www.KimandJason.com © 2004 by Jason W. Kotecki
No, I mean about my outfit. Does it look okay?

"Do I look sparkly? I stole some of Katie's body glitter because I'm a star." -- Kim

I'm off to bat, boys!
www.KimandJason.com © 2004 by Jason W. Kotecki
Watch me hit one over the fence!
Kotecki
I guess it won't be too hard if she faces THAT direction.
Not if that's how she holds the bat.

I can't BELIEVE he called me out!
YOU'RE BLIND, UMP!
www.KimandJason.com © 2004 by Jason W. Kotecki
Kim, everybody here saw you tackle the first baseman.
He wouldn't get his foot off MY base!
Kotecki

"...and then he kept touching me with his stupid glove!" -- Kim

OK EVERYBODY-- LISTEN UP!
I'm going to hit it now, and I'd appreciate it if you didn't catch it this time.
Thanks.
Kotecki
www.KimandJason.com © 2004 by Jason W. Kotecki

Childhood IS...
Playing The Game YOUR Way.
STAY AWAY
www.KimandJason.com © 2004 by Jason W. Kotecki
I can tell your friend Kim has never played baseball before...
She made it to second base, but she still has the bat.
Yes, but look how the fielders keep their distance.
kotecki

"Who knew a home run could be so easy...and violent." -- Jason

Hey, how come that ump keeps going over to talk to the other team?
He's their coach.
www.KimandJason.com © 2004 by Jason W. Kotecki
WHAT?! It's a conspiracy! This game is rigged!
Our coach is an ump, too.
He is?
Give him a five spot and see if he'll give me one of those home runs.
kotecki

"What do you think he'll give me for a dime? I think I have a dime." -- Kim

Oh man, why did the coach stick me way out here?
www.KimandJason.com © 2004 by Jason W. Kotecki
Heck, I can't even SEE anybody from out here.
Nobody will ever hit it this far...
!
OH! -- There they all are!
kotecki

"Wait...why is everybody on my team sitting on the bench?" -- Kim

www.KimandJason.com © 2004 by Jason W. Kotecki
Hey! What are you doing? You're supposed to be playing right field!
It's **BORING** over there.
Kotecki

"I'm surprised they don't call it boring field. I wonder if they'll let me bring a Slip 'N Slide out here..." -- Kim

C'MON GUYS! LET'S GET SOME OUTS!
www.KimandJason.com © 2004 by Jason W. Kotecki
If I stay out here any longer, I'm gonna end up on a milk carton!

"These kids on my team really stink. Maybe I should let them borrow my glove – theirs seem to be broken." -- Kim

Playing outfield **STINKS**.
Nobody ever hits it to me.
CRACK
www.KimandJason.com © 2004 by Jason W. Kotecki
Either it's too short or too far.
Kotecki

Childhood Is...
Playing The Outfield.
www.KimandJason.com © 2004 by Jason W. Kotecki
Hey– second base kid!
How 'bout getting me some water?
Kotecki

kotecki
www.KimandJason.com © 2004 by Jason W. Kotecki

A Day In The Life Of A T-Ball Outfielder.

This is it. We need one more run to win.
www.KimandJason.com © 2004 by Jason W. Kotecki
HIT
kotecki
I DID IT! I got a hit! I didn't let the team down!
I wonder where the post game press conference will be...

I'm the winning run!
But first I have to make it to second base.
That kid covering the bag looks pretty big.
www.KimandJason.com © 2004 by Jason W. Kotecki
I TOLD Mom I needed those metal cleats!
kotecki

I made it to third base!
If I score, we win the game! Two outs – who's up?
Kotecki
Oh no – It's **KIM**!
www.KimandJason.com © 2004 by Jason W. Kotecki
I hope you're all ready for a game-winning touchdown!

It all comes down to this. If Kim gets a hit – we win!
OMigosh! SHE HIT IT!
www.KimandJason.com © 2004 by Jason W. Kotecki
That's a good one! And she remembered to run to first, too!
YER OUT!
TAG
But I forgot to run home...
Kotecki

"So this is what goats feel like." -- Jason

I can't believe I blew the game for the team...
I let **EVERYBODY** down.
How can I ever face them?
I don't think you have to worry about that...
www.KimandJason.com © 2004 by Jason W. Kotecki
We got snacks!

Childhood Is...
Snack After T-Ball.
www.KimandJason.com © 2004 by Jason W. Kotecki
Oreos® **AND** orange drink?
I **LOVE** baseball!
Kotecki

Let's get this fireworks show on the road!
Hey, I OFFERED to go see if they needed any help, but you heard my Mom.
She's SO unpatriotic.
kotecki
www.KimandJason.com © 2004 by Jason W. Kotecki

THE CHALK ARTISTS

Ah, sidewalk chalk, nothing quite like it. It doesn't get much respect in the world of Renaissance oil painting and ancient frescos, but it's sure reminiscent of childhood, is it not? I always wished the colors were a bit bolder, but I enjoyed my duty of beautifying those drab concrete slabs in front of my house. Were my creations as heralded or appreciated as a Van Gogh? Probably not, but I never cut off my own ear, either.

Wanna do some chalk drawings with me?
Sure!
Let's go out to the sidewalk.
Kotecki
www.KimandJason.com © 2004 by Jason W. Kotecki
I'm already finished with the basement floor.

Looks like we're stuck with what we've got.
www.KimandJason.com © 2004 by Jason W. Kotecki
It's chalk or nothing.
Your Mom wouldn't let us use the permanent marker?
Nope. And I guess spray paint is out, too.
Kotecki

It's nice to draw on the sidewalk instead of paper for a change.
www.KimandJason.com © 2004 by Jason W. Kotecki
Yeah.
Kotecki
Hey - Do you think God gets upset about us coloring all over his stuff?

Do we have any brown chalk left?
www.KimandJason.com © 2004 by Jason W. Kotecki
Um, nope, no brown.
Great. I guess now I'll have to make my trees orange.
I don't think anyone will notice, what with all the teal and fuchsia houses.
kotecki

HEY!
This is ART!
Sorry – my bad.
kotecki
www.KimandJason.com © 2004 by Jason W. Kotecki
If this was a PICASSO, she'd get arrested.
Well this isn't a McCasso, but it IS a KIM!
Do you think we could at least get her handcuffed?

Shall not the simple chalk drawings of a child be considered high art?
Why not, I say?
They possess all of the expressiveness of a Van Gogh...
And they're abstract enough to welcome individual interpretation...
What is that, an ambulance?
No, silly! It's a clown riding a horse with two chickens!
kotecki
See, this slab of concrete should be worth twenty to thirty thousand, easy.
www.KimandJason.com © 2004 by Jason W. Kotecki

Childhood IS ...
Drawing On The Sidewalk.
www.KimandJason.com © 2004 by Jason W. Kotecki
YIKES. I need an eraser.
Either that, or your Dad needs a smaller head.
kotecki

"Either that, or your dad needs a smaller head."

Jason, how about taking out the garbage?
www.KimandJason.com © 2004 by Jason W. Kotecki
You can't MAKE me.
kotecki
My Dad is good at making things.

Mom, can I be done cleaning my room?
Is it finished?
www.KimandJason.com © 2004 by Jason W. Kotecki
Not all the way, but I've been working for HOURS.
You've been in there for 10 minutes. Now get going.
Perhaps we should forego the round of Candyland this time.
kotecki

Stinky Speaks

Ironically, the only thing the diversion of Candyland® accomplished was to make the room even more messy. That, and it confirmed my deep-seated hate for the game, especially when played with a deck of only five cards.

Oh MAN!
kotecki
www.KimandJason.com © 2004 by Jason W. Kotecki
Broccoli AGAIN?!
I'm not eating this POISON!
If lemon broccoli risoto is poison, I'll die a happy skunk.
Here, hide this under your tail.

BELLLCH
kotecki
www.KimandJason.com © 2004 by Jason W. Kotecki
KIM! Where are your manners?
They're still playing outside.

Boompa, do you know what a mermaid is?
Yes - it's a mythical creature that's half woman and half fish.
www.KimandJason.com © 2004 by Jason W. Kotecki
YIKES. I bet she's pretty ugly.
kotecki
They're supposed to be quite beautiful, actually.
BEAUTIFUL? With the head of a FISH?

Childhood IS...
Brutal Honesty.
www.KimandJason.com © 2004 by Jason W. Kotecki
Boompa, if you don't lie a lot, how the heck did your nose get so big?
kotecki

Childhood Is...
Youthful Energy.
www.KimandJason.com © 2004 by Jason W. Kotecki
No-YOU'VE got the cootie cablooies- no tag backs!
If somebody could bottle that, coffee growers would be out of business.
kotecki

I never would have thought it possible...
...But lipstick manufacturers have managed to invent 53,074 different shades of red.
www.KimandJason.com © 2004 by Jason W. Kotecki
I wonder how many shades of green they're up to...
Hey - have you seen the cap to this marker?
kotecki

THE HOW-TO BOOK

Who better to write a how-to book about being a superhero than Super J? (I mean *besides* the entire pantheon of Marvel® and DC® luminaries.) Perhaps none of them had the foresight to fill such a glaring need in the market-place, perhaps they were too busy with actual crime fighting. Whatever the case may be, I had a super fun time writing this episode. My favorite strip? Probably the one about the book signing.

Talk about disappointing.
kotecki
An entire library and not ONE book on how to be a superhero!
SNAKES
www.KimandJason.com © 2004 by Jason W. Kotecki
I'd think there'd be at least two.
No wonder you don't see any superheroes these days.

Why haven't any superheroes written any books?
Maybe they're all too busy.
ZIP
kotecki
Can you fetch me some paper, miss?
I guess not ALL of them are busy.
www.KimandJason.com © 2004 by Jason W. Kotecki
Fortunately it's a light crime day...
and it's raining outside.

Super J's Super Secret Log #000036

I'm not afraid of the rain - no way. I'm not afraid of anything.

But when I go outside in the rain, my cape gets all soggy, and it weighs me down.

How to Be A Superhero
Chapter 1
Be born with at least one or two amazing powers.
If that doesn't work, get involved in some sort of nuclear accident.
www.KimandJason.com © 2004 by Jason W. Kotecki
kotecki

Super J's Super Secret Log #000037

Another solution would be to take after Batman (a good friend of mine). He wasn't born with any super powers. He just worked out, studied hard, and made all kinds of cool gadgets for hiself in his spare time.

But that's a lot of work.

So how is the book coming?
kotecki
www.KimandJason.com © 2004 by Jason W. Kotecki
GOOD! I'm writing about uniforms right now.
As you can see, mine is the classic style...
Cape, logo, boots...
Ask him if the underpants NEED to be inside out.

Super J's Super Secret Log #000038

Someday, I'd like to upgrade to some sort of rubber molded suit that shows off all my big muscles. Those kind are all the rage these days. And maybe it could add a few extra here and there.

How to Be A Superhero
Chapter 3
Step One: Find out yer weekniss (Like KriptoNITE)
StEp 2: Stay away from it.
StEp 3: Repeat Step Two.
www.KimandJason.com © 2004 by Jason W. Kotecki
kotecki

Super J's Super Secret Log #000039

Some superheroes, like me, don't really have too many weaknesses. I'm 'lergic to Kryptonite, but I don't see it around very much where I live.

Sometimes I've found it hidden in girl's perfume. That stuff is nasty, and I try and stay away from it at all costs.

Childhood Is...
Heroic Occupations.
www.KimandJason.com © 2004 by Jason W. Kotecki
It's a lot of hard work, but being a superhero is a very rewarding job.
Who can argue with job benefits like x-ray vision and vehicles that make James Bond's ride look like a rusted out Reliant?
kotecki

Super J's Super Secret Log #000040

It's a good feeling to help people who can't help themselves because they don't have any super powers like I do.

I also think it would be a good feeling to see somebody make a movie about me someday.

I'm trying to find a cover photo for my book "How to Be A Superhero."
How 'bout this one where you're choking the teddy bear?
That's not really my good side.
train
www.KimandJason.com © 2004 by Jason W. Kotecki
kotecki

How to Be A Superhero
Chapter 4
Sekret Idendidy.
It's important to maintane two idendidies.
Jason! Take out the trash!
Sorry, no Jason here!
I've found it has many advantigis.
www.KimandJason.com © 2004 by Jason W. Kotecki
kotecki

Super J's Super Secret Log #000041

The thing that makes my identity really secret is the glasses. No one can tell who I really am with these glasses on. It's impossible.

How did I come up with such a good idea, you ask? It seemed to work out really good for Superman, so I just reversed it.

ALL FINISHED!
www.KimandJason.com © 2004 by Jason W. Kotecki
I've revealed everything it takes to be a top-notch superhero.
And another selfless act to benefit mankind is under my belt.
So the book is free, then?
Heck no— $19.95 Superheroes have bills too.

Super J's Super Secret Log #000042

Of course superheroes have bills!

Where do people think all the fancy utility belts, super vehicles, and secret hideouts come from? That stuff doesn't grow on trees, you know.

Well, my hideout kind of does...it's a treehouse.

Book Signing to-day!
Book Signing to-day!
www.KimandJason.com © 2004 by Jason W. Kotecki
Book Signing to-day!
Did a new Harry Potter book come out today or something?
Book Signing to-day!
kotecki

Super J's Super Secret Log #000043

I've been sitting here for a few hours now, and no autograph seekers. Either a new Harry Potter book just came out or I just found out another reason superheroes need agents.

At least Batman has a butler.

Hello, little girl, would you like an autographed copy of my book?
Book Signing to-day!
No. Your Mom wants to know if you want a grilled cheese or a ham samwich.
Hmmm...that's interesting.
www.KimandJason.com © 2004 by Jason W. Kotecki
My Mother was tragically killed when my home planet of Nebulon exploded.
Grilled cheese it is, then.
kotecki

Super J's Super Secret Log #000044

I thought for sure that little fair-haired girl would want a signed copy of my new book. I think she was intimidated by seeing me live and in person. Maybe she felt embarrassed about bringing up the tragedy about my Mom. It was nice of her to offer to bring me a grilled cheese samwich. I hope it doesn't upset her further when she finds out Super J is blacktoast intolerant.

What's this? "How To Be A Super-hero"?
Yes... you wrote the thing, remember?
ME?
This was written by SUPER J.
www.KimandJason.com © 2004 by Jason W. Kotecki
This guy has some real talent. isn't he AMAZING?
You're still wearing your boots.
kotecki

Super J's Super Secret Log #000045

It's nice to know that I have fans all over the place. This Jason fellow seems like a real swell guy. I wonder why the little fair-haired girl doesn't pay more attention to his good sense.

And I wonder where he was during my book signing.

Childhood Is...
SUPER-SIZED Solutions To Everyday Problems.
www.KimandJason.com © 2004 by Jason W. Kotecki
Shoot. I broke an egg.
Would you like me to reverse the Earth's rotation so you can go back in time and prevent the accident?
If for some reason that fails, I vote for paper towels as a back-up plan.

Super J's Super Secret Log #000046

Sometimes I have so many super powers that people don't even stop and think how much I could help them. I can't blame them. Sometimes I forget a super power now and then. Heck, just today I rediscovered my ability to find a cereal box prize without spilling any cereal from the box.

Kim & Jason
by kotecki
Have you ever thought about what you'd buy if you won the lottery?
Two ponies, a pink convertible, a big castle, a bi-plane with my name on it, a princess gown with diamond sparkles, a drum set, and of course, a dog.
I'll take that as a yes...
And I'd buy warm chocolate chip cookies with whatever's left.
kotecki
www.KimandJason.com © 2004 by Jason W. Kotecki

Boompa, smoke alarms help keep people safe if there's a fire, right?
That's right.
Let's fire up that burner – we're safe!
kotecki
© 2004 by Jason W. Kotecki
www.KimandJason.com

Hey look, a dead bird.
He might be dead from pollution.
Really?
God smokes?
kotecki
www.KimandJason.com © 2004 by Jason W. Kotecki

Hey, look! I found a bottle cap!
Quick–check to see if you won!
It says, "Sorry, try again."
I'm not even sure what I was trying to win...
We'll find out soon enough...
Now do what it says–put it back down so I can try.
kotecki
www.KimandJason.com © 2004 by Jason W. Kotecki

I'm making a list of all the things I want banned from the Earth.
Your sister Katie is on the list, right?
OMIGOSH! I almost forgot about her!
She's up to number one with a bullet!
Take that, wet socks!
kotecki
www.KimandJason.com © 2004 by Jason W. Kotecki

How's the list of things you want banned from the Earth?
www.KimandJason.com © 2004 by Jason W. Kotecki
Pretty good! So far, Ive got down Katie, wet socks, broccoli, and chores.
You know, it might be hard to get these things banned from the WHOLE EARTH.
kotecki
I know, but I'd be happy if we started with them being banned from ME.

I have to go to the bathroom.
Use the one upstairs. This one's broke.
What happened to you?
kotecki
www.KimandJason.com
Kim & Jason
by kotecki
I just walked in on Katie.
What, was she naked or something?
No, but she had a huge towel on her head...
And whip cream all over her LEGS!
You need a sister.
And there was this HORRIBLE smell...
Bath salts?
It was NASTY.
© 2004 by Jason W. Kotecki

AssortiD Hair Cair ProduKs 25¢
www.KimandJason.com © 2004 by Jason W. Kotecki
This brush is actually pretty nice...
Only 25¢
So are these barrettes - WAIT.- This is all MY stuff!
Wait 'till she hears we sold her hair dryer.
We'll give her a commission.
kotecki